D0897630

NEGOTIATE
·LIKE THE·
PROS

Other Books by the Author

Agents of Opportunity: Sports Agents and Corruption in Collegiate Sports

In Black and White: Race and Sports in America

The Sports Franchise Game: Cities in Pursuit of Sports Franchises, Events, Stadiums, and Arenas

Basketball Jones: America, Above the Rim

The Business of Sports

The Business of Sports Agents

Being Sugar Ray: America's Greatest Boxer and First Celebrity Athlete

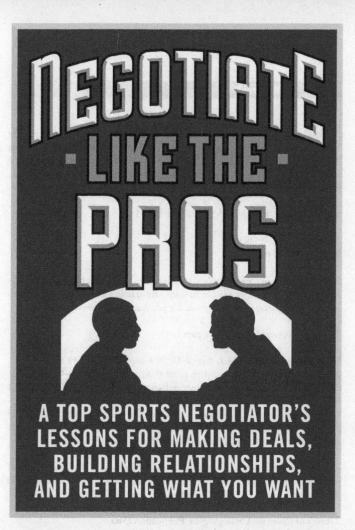

NEGOTIATE
· LIKE THE ·
PROS

A TOP SPORTS NEGOTIATOR'S LESSONS FOR MAKING DEALS, BUILDING RELATIONSHIPS, AND GETTING WHAT YOU WANT

KENNETH L. SHROPSHIRE

New York   Chicago   San Francisco   Lisbon   London
Madrid   Mexico City   Milan   New Delhi   San Juan
Seoul   Singapore   Sydney   Toronto

1 2 3 4 5 6 7 8 9 0   QVS/QVS   6 5 4 3

ISBN   978-0-07-154831-1
MHID 0-07-154831-9

McGraw-Hill books are available at special quantity discounts to use as premiums and sales promotions, or for use in corporate training programs. To contact a representative please visit the Contact Us pages at www.mhprofessional.com.

This book is printed on acid-free paper.

Photo credits: p. 27 © Andy Lyons–Getty Images Sport; p. 49 © Ronald C. Modra/Sports–Getty Images Sport; p. 59 © Matthew Stockman–Getty Images Sport; p. 79 © Alexander Hassenstein–Bongarts; p. 92 © AFP–AFP; p. 111 © Chad Buchanan–Getty Images Entertainment; p. 113 © Victor Decolongon–Getty Images Sport; 135 © Transcendental Graphics–Getty Images Sport; p. 139 © Vernon Biever–National Football League; p. 155 © Mark Wilson–Getty Images News; p. 168 © Al Messerschmidt–Getty Images Sport

The Bargaining Styles Assessment Tool in the Appendix is reprinted with permission from G. Richard Shell, *Bargaining for Advantage: Negotiation Strategies for Reasonable People,* Appendix A (New York, Penguin, 2nd edition, 2006).

Library of Congress Cataloging-in-Publication Data
Shropshire, Kenneth L.
  Negotiate like the pros / by Kenneth L. Shropshire.
      p. cm.
  Includes bibliographical references and index.
  ISBN-13: 978-0-07-154831-1 (alk. paper)
  ISBN-10: 0-07-154831-9 (alk. paper)
  1. Negotiation in business. 2. Negotiations. I. Title.
  HD58.6.S574 2009
  658.4'052—dc22

                                                                2008036865

For my favorite athletes, Theresa, Sam, and Diane.
Also in memory of Brandon Walker,
who left us all much too soon.

CONTENTS

ACKNOWLEDGMENTS

There are many people to thank for their assistance and support on this book. Those whom I formally interviewed are cited in the notes. Their time is valuable, and I appreciate the amount that they were able to give to me. I have also gained insight from the many people with whom I've discussed this topic over the years and from those whom I observed along the way. Those people are too numerous to name here, but among them are my fellow board members on the Sports Lawyers Association, a group that, in my opinion, includes some of the finest negotiators in the world.

Projects such as this book never come to completion for me without a strong core of student researchers. Over the course of writing, those people have included Colleen Baker, Amanda Bensol, Jon Gantman, Ryan Mallory, Cory Moelis, Stephon Murray, Calvin Otis, Matty Tellem, and Alex Valner.

Thanks to my Wharton Sports Business Initiative colleagues Charles Grantham, Scott Rosner, and Mori

Taheripour for assistance with various parts of the manuscript. Thanks also to the Legal Studies and Business Ethics research fund, which provided some of the seed funding to get this project underway. Thanks to Ashley Fox for helpful insights on some of the football-related deals.

At McGraw-Hill, I particularly want to thank Leah Spiro and Colin Kelly, the first true believers in the book, as well as others who did the work that results in a finished product, including Janice Race, Morgan Ertel, Kenya Henderson, and Gaya Vinay. Thanks also to my colleague Jerry Wind, who was key in prompting me to write the proposal for this book in the first place.

Thanks to Stanford Business School professor Margaret Neale for being kind enough several years ago to allow me to take an executive negotiation course with her and alongside some amazing businesspeople. I went to Stanford to increase my understanding of how to teach my negotiation course, and I could not have had better guidance by example. Her thoughts and her work, especially *Negotiating Rationally*, have surely made their way into this book. I mention my colleague Richard Shell in a few key places in this book. He was extremely generous when I first began to work in the area of negotiating and has continued to be so throughout.

Finally, thanks to all of the students, whether executives, high schoolers, athletes, or others who have attended my courses over the years. Often I have learned much more from you than you realize. To all of those who helped me with this project, I give you credit for all that is positive, and I of course take responsibility for any shortcomings.

INTRODUCTION
HOW AND WHY TO USE THIS BOOK

If you don't know where you're going,
you'll end up somewhere else.

—Yogi Berra, baseball Hall of Famer

Do you want to be a better negotiator? Do you want to negotiate with the same success and confidence that you see among the professionals who handle the business of teams, leagues, athletes, and others in the sports pages and on ESPN on a daily basis? If you want to become stellar at deal making, building relationships, persuasion, and even leadership, this book is for you—sports fan or not.

I teach negotiations at the Wharton School of Business as well as to executives at locations around the world. I also negotiate for real. From Fortune 500 companies to sports leagues, agents, athletes, boxing promoters, team executives, and big- and little-city mayors, I've had a broad range of experiences with a variety of business deals. I tell you about some of them in this book.

This book provides an approach that challenges you to mentally analyze your own negotiating techniques, style, relationship-building strategies, and powers of persuasion and compare these with other people's. When you're done reading it, whether you're an executive or a student, an athlete or a sports fan, you will become a better negotiator. And with practice, you will be even better still. If you're in a sports business setting, great, but most readers will never apply any of this in the realm of sports at all. Most of you will use these negotiating principles in business as well as in your personal lives, just as I do. This book focuses on more than just deal making. It readjusts your focus to the importance of relationship building, even if there is not a traditional transaction in sight. There is an overriding philosophy that resonates among those who think about negotiating that says: if you have not groomed a relationship before you need it, it's probably too late.

Most people who will casually pick up this book will be just like I used to be. I thought either you could negotiate well or you couldn't, and that was the end of it. Certainly, I reasoned, negotiating could not be *taught*, as the advertisements declared in so many airline magazines over the years. I was convinced that you could not successfully copy the styles of these bargaining book and workshop-selling gurus.

Then, two decades ago, a colleague of mine at Wharton, Richard Shell, began teaching a course called Negotiation and Dispute Resolution. He suggested that I might give teaching it a try, but at the time it was not for me. And then, a few years back—more as a change of pace from my regular sports-business teaching regimen than from any great epiphany—I decided to take a shot at teaching negotiations. I proceeded to immerse myself in negotiations literature and instruction. Frankly, I was amazed at what I found. I am now convinced that anyone can be taught to be a better negotiator.

I'm still consistent in my belief that you cannot be *taught* to dramatically *change* your negotiating style—to become someone else. As a matter of fact, I think an overhaul of your style could be one of the worst moves you could make. But you can be taught to *understand* your style and to be *better* at what you are comfortable doing. This is more a focus on a change of techniques and steps as opposed to hopeless attempts to reform your entire personality. You can be taught to use the skills that you have to become a better negotiator. You can learn how to focus those tools into a systematic style and method and to go beyond traditional deals by building relationships. What I am referring to is an organized approach to negotiating. The overall key to success is to first understand *you*. Then, gather as much information as possible about *your counterpart*. Finally, prepare a game plan and follow through with it, making relevant adjustments along the way.

In this book, I take you through the preparation and execution of that game plan. I do so by capturing various negotiations related to the business of sports. Many of the stories will be told through the voices of people actually involved in the deals. The deals are one part of what we'll look at. We will also focus on the broader relationship lessons that come from sports and how to incorporate those into your relationship dealings with people. So I don't just look at deal makers and athletes but also at sports motivators who provoke the achievement of many amazing athletic feats. The winning techniques of people like legendary coaches John Wooden and Pat Summitt loom large in sports and can often be transferred to business as well as to your personal lives. There is much to be learned from coaches who have developed successful strategies to inspire men and women, sometimes with outsized egos, to do exactly what they want them to do.

I could have chosen a variety of stories to convey these messages. I carefully selected and synthesized the ones that deliver the lessons that will lead you to greater bargaining success. I incorporate figures from around the world, such as David Beckham, Yao Ming, Pelé, Danica Patrick, Daisuke Matsuzaka, Ronaldo, and Anna Kournikova, and sports, including cricket, the Olympics, rugby, golf, and tennis. I use stories involving sports agents, lawyers, and union and management officials as well.

I also discuss some of my own negotiations. Most of them did not find their way to the cover of major newspapers, but they provide vivid insights nonetheless. They had a meaningful impact on the way I negotiate, especially as I ponder them and reflect on how I can improve. I look back on my own experiences with this in mind, and you should too.

You can be a better negotiator. The key to gaining value from this book is committing yourself to taking an introspective look and accepting the reality of what you find. My offensive line coach at Stanford University, Hudson Houck, in a rare moment of paying attention to a guy who was then a very undersized center, yelled at me once when I blew (yet another) play in football practice:

"Dammit, Shropshire, you're not that big, not that fast, and not that strong. Hell, you've got to play smart." The man had a point. His intended message was: use what you've got, because you can't create something you don't have . . . at least not overnight. If you at least harness that strong point, you can make yourself the best player you can be. Well, as was evidenced by my lack of playing time over four years, at the time I did not get it. His attempt at inspiring greater achievement out of me fell a little short. Hopefully, you will be more open-minded and receptive to the messages in this book.

So take this step forward toward more successful negotiations. Here is what the book delivers.

Chapter 1, "Prepare with Passion," focuses on the most important element in any negotiation: preparation. You'll understand both how to prepare and why taking the time to do so can be the most valuable transformation you can make in your negotiating life. That viewpoint dominates in sports, and it should be just as prevalent in business dealings. There are many coaching admonitions that dwell on the phrase "just do your job." The unstated obvious precursor to that point is that you have to know what that job is. You'll refer back to this chapter once you have a better grasp of the focused negotiation issues presented in the chapters that follow, and eventually you'll be able to thoroughly prepare with the assistance of the Negotiation Game Plan Worksheet provided in this chapter.

The next chapter, "Stick with *Your* Style," guides you through both understanding your most comfortable bargaining style as well as how to use it to your advantage rather than fretting about a style that does not come easily to you. In sports, we most often express this as "playing within yourself." As a part of your journey, I will refer you at that point in the book to the appendix containing the Bargaining Styles Assessment Tool, reprinted from Richard Shell's negotiation book called *Bargaining for Advantage*. At the appropriate time, the text will instruct you to take this 10-minute assessment to help you fully grasp your style.

The third chapter, "Set Goals and Aim High," relays the value of establishing goals and making them a regular part of your preparation process. It is not unusual for sports teams to begin a season aiming for an event or for the Olympics by setting goals for the number and types of medals they will win. It is clear that the higher your goals are and the more support you have for them, the more successful you are likely to be.

Chapter 4, "Seek Leverage," explores how lying and negotiating somehow seem to go hand in hand. It helps you push back against lying while focusing on the topic that is lied about most: tales told to create leverage. In sports and non-sports negotiations, the most prevalent lie is about how interested potential bidders really are in your goods or services.

Chapter 5, "Focus on Relationships and Interests," takes you beyond the monetary side of deals and focuses your attention on the other benefits that flow from them. For an athlete, such a side benefit may be a supportive relationship with the hometown crowd, as opposed to moving to a new city as a free agent for more money. In business, this benefit may be likened to a long-term relationship with a vendor or boss.

"Embrace the Bargaining Process," the sixth chapter, guides you to the mental level of enjoyment that you should strive to achieve in negotiating. Practice in sports is often drudgery, and so too may be the preparation required for a negotiation. But when you actually are at bat or when the Sunday event actually comes around, that should be a time of sheer enjoyment. Ideally, the same should be true for preparation, as well as for the various other phases of the negotiation process.

At some point, almost all of us are on one end or the other of an employer-employee negotiation. Or we may be negotiating for someone else or hiring someone to negotiate for us, which also raises issues of negotiating with business partners. Chapter 7, "Handle Other People's Business," focuses on player-agent negotiations and relationships. You will better understand how to negotiate on behalf of a company or an individual, as well as how to manage someone negotiating on your behalf. The chapter also provides some insights on negotiations that can help you to build relationships that work on both a personal and a business level.

Although it does not happen often, the one negotiation we should all be prepared for is the one that takes place in full view of the public. The public venue can be anywhere from a small company setting to the national stage. Most often negotiations within the public eye focus on your reputation or your company's. The sports business is full of this type of negotiation. In the eighth chapter, "Know Your Audience," I look at issues such as steroids in baseball, as well as the saga of Michael Vick and dog fighting. In your case, the audience may be smaller—maybe just your family, coworkers, or classmates.

Finally, the concluding chapter, "Negotiate Like a Pro," ties all of the elements together and assists you in doing just that.

"Smart wins" is a favorite saying of college basketball coach Bobby Knight. I've heard him shout those two words angrily to players in the midst of a game or practice. In essence, he's saying: "I'm not asking you to do anything more than the best you are capable of, and I know you know what that is." Increased success using the skills that you possess will come with greater understanding of what those skills are and how to use them. "Smart wins" puts you in the best position to win. That's what Hudson was trying to tell me.

⇥ Takeaways ⇤

Getting Started

1. Commit to taking a new, organized approach to negotiating.
2. Be open to understanding and criticizing yourself in this process.
3. Be prepared to focus on the steps that you will take *before* beginning the negotiation.
4. Focus on developing your Negotiation Game Plan Worksheet.

Don't

1. Assume you know it all.
2. Go on to the next page without being open to change.

CHAPTER 1

PREPARE WITH PASSION

Failing to prepare is preparing to fail.

—Legendary coach John Wooden, winner of
10 National Collegiate Athletic Association
(NCAA) basketball championships

"The Soviets are boycotting," Danny Villanueva, the commissioner of the Olympic boxing competition, pulled me aside to tell me. "You know that means we won't have Cuba." This was bad news because I was in charge of boxing's day-to-day operations in the 1984 Olympics. The Los Angeles Olympic Organizing Committee had been housed in the cavernous former Bell helicopter factory for just a few months—a physical move made to accommodate the ever-increasing games' planning staff.

Now, if what Villanueva said did come to pass, the absence of the legendary heavyweight Teófilo Stevenson and the rest of the Cuban boxing team, loaded with talent, was going to be a huge blow to the quality of the games as well as the morale of our staff. This was our narrow focus, but the absence of the Cuban baseball team and all the Soviet sports teams would be devastating.

Peter Ueberroth, the head of the Los Angeles Organizing Committee, was determined to get the Cuban team to come to the 1984 Games in Los Angeles. If Ueberroth was to be successful, the key was convincing Fidel Castro not to join the Olympic boycott that was being initiated by the Soviet Union, then a world superpower. And that depended on how well Ueberroth was prepared for the negotiation with Castro.

Political and crucial economic ties between Cuba and the Soviet Union made convincing the island nation to come to Los Angeles look like an impossible dream. The negotiation was to incorporate more than just Cuba's participation in the games. The conversation had to be sensitive to the vestiges of the 30-year cozy cold war relationship between Russia and Cuba, where Cubans traveled to Russia to study and Russians came to Cuba to work as technicians and soldiers. Ueberroth had to understand clearly the Soviet omnipresence in Cuba during that era as memorialized in the first names Svetlana and Vladimir of so many Cubans, in addition to the presence of the old boxy Soviet Lada sedans and Ural motorcycles. This was not going to be easy. But it was a goal being pursued by the man who would in the coming year be named *Time* magazine's "Man of the Year" after the wildly successful 1984 Olympics.

Of all the people I've met in sports over the years and had firsthand dealings with, Ueberroth is to be given credit for being the best negotiator I've seen in action. There was certainly a great deal of gravitas and situational leverage on his side in the moments when I saw him at work and was working on his behalf. But his success in negotiating inside of sports was undeniable.

His secret? In my mind the real source of his success was relentless preparation. He demanded that his staff never put themselves, and certainly never put him, in a position where they were surprised by any transaction. In any setting, that is a lofty ambition. In what was essentially a global sports venture, it was even more so. Were we always successful? No. But the lack of success was usually because the deal, whatever it was, just could not be made, not because our homework was incomplete.

That preparation was intense on the personal level and in the way Ueberroth infused the entire organization with the need to be prepared. Even in secretarial positions, you had to know the Olympics and the people you were likely to deal with, the global sports community.

This knowledge was not merely assumed. Ueberroth personally tested new hires on the history of the Olympics during their first week on the job. I'm not kidding. He would call the new hires into a conference room. After a cordial welcome to the 15 or so new hires at a rectangular conference table, he might open with "what is the last foreign country you visited?" and in a rapid fire manner he'd look at each of the new staffers for a response. "Mexico" or "Canada" received little notice. If you said

"Yugoslavia," he might pause and ask you what you thought about some recent political event there, and he'd look at you with disgust if you had no or an inadequate response. Then, he would, elementary-school style, pass out an exam with questions like "where were the first Olympic Games held?" and "name every Olympic city that begins with the letter M" and "name the [then] twenty-three Olympic sports." The political questions included "what is the leading newspaper in Moscow?" and "what is the official name of East Germany?" The message was clear, especially for the poor performers on those tests: you never know when you will be representing the Olympic Organizing Committee and when even your casual interaction with someone else from the Olympic world can have an impact on a major transaction.

The atmosphere was heavy with the knowledge that a big part of the business was the *relationship* business, and knowledge—knowledge of one's counterparts and adversaries—was the key to successful relationships.

That was the atmosphere in which we worked. When the boycott announcement came, insiders knew that Ueberroth would negotiate directly with Castro. His staffers wrote a report that told him: "The key to successfully meeting with him [Castro] is to remember that he is a monologist, often [talking] nonstop for an hour or two. He loves to lecture and will do so on any subject, sometimes not the one which is the particular subject for the meeting." This was solid information, and it presented a tough task for Ueberroth, who was not short on ego himself, although not to those

Castro extremes. He'd done the appropriate homework; now, what to do with it?

Early in the morning when the report was due, I added what I could to a separate report that Dr. Harvey Schiller had prepared. Schiller, who was at that time an Air Force colonel on loan to the committee to work with me in boxing, put together a document that reflected his background, including details about the airfield on which Ueberroth's delegation would be likely to land. Schiller, too, with a military background as a pilot in Vietnam as well as a doctorate in chemistry, was a master at detail. He knew what Ueberroth needed, and he delivered in a way that only his military and chemistry background could provide. All the people involved had come to understand that the fewer surprises, the greater the likelihood of success in the negotiation.

At the time this was occurring, I was in my mid-twenties. Admittedly, all of this was pretty heady stuff. Yesterday the Soviets and Cubans were entities I had only read about. Today I was involved in how to beat them at the bargaining table. If it was not clear to me before then, it was crystal clear to me now that successful people do not "wing it" if they don't have to. They are successful for many reasons, and preparing, not allowing themselves to get blindsided, is one of them. That lesson would be reinforced over and over again as I moved forward in the sports world.

The guidance Ueberroth received about the Cuban leader went on: "If it is clear that he is in a monologue mood, let him go, don't interrupt. Sometimes, he is open to dialogue at once. You have to be the judge of the situation." This provided Ueberroth with plan A and the appropriate cue for when to proceed to plan B.

To prepare, you must know beforehand what you absolutely must have, what it would be fair to have, and what would be great to have. More formally, I refer to these as my walk-away points, targets, and goals. The bigger plan outlines how to get there. You have to view a negotiation as a cross-country road race, where the course is not seen in advance, as compared to a sprint, where the track is pristine and all you need to do is to go straight ahead as fast as possible.

The report provided Ueberroth even greater insight into Castro's personality. It read, "Flattery is useful with anyone, but particularly so with [Castro]—his own sports prowess, the strength of his athletes under his leadership, etc."

As is the case today, there were myths and realities about Castro's athletic career, including one story that he had had a tryout with the New York Yankees (an alternative tale says the Washington Senators) as a left-handed pitcher. Would Castro say it is true?

CULTURAL, GENDER, AND RACIAL DIFFERENCES

It was clear to all that Castro viewed sports as an important element for his country's well-being. A big part of the preparation for the meeting with Castro was an understanding of the Cuban culture. Ueberroth, the former travel agency executive, was a student of cultures and was naturally prepared at that level.

With any global negotiation, you *must* take the time to learn and understand the negotiating style of the culture of your negotiating partner. At the same time, you *must not* view any of the descriptions you find as absolute. Just as you wouldn't like to be stereotyped as an "American-style" negotiator, those in other cultures also do not want to be stereotyped. Be aware, but do not assume. For example, there may be a deal maker from China who has adopted the style she learned while studying at the Harvard Business School. She may choose not to spend long hours of socializing to get to know you, and she really wants to get the deal done as soon as possible and head back to Beijing.

Most negotiation books reserve a special section for the topic of "cross-cultural negotiations" or "the impact of gender." I'll discuss some specifics later. But what the business of sports makes you keenly aware of is that every negotiation is potentially cross-cultural or contains gender issues, even if all of the principals are from the same city and of the same gender. It's easy to know you need to have a grasp of cultural issues when you are negotiating with the parents of an 18-year-old Dominican baseball player. But you would be wise to have a similar awareness of the cultural uniqueness of the potential Women's National Basketball Association (WNBA) star raised on a farm in

Nebraska, or of the billionaire who owns the golf course where you want to host your charity event.

Similarly, when you are recruiting a male athlete, if his mother is the gatekeeper in terms of the final decision about whether or not to let you represent him, you had better consider issues specifically related to her. Know as much as you can about the style, culture, gender, and idiosyncrasies of your counterpart, and don't reserve that focus solely for those times when you are boarding an overseas flight, dialing an international number, or dealing with someone of the opposite sex. Let's be honest, too: if you are negotiating in the United States with someone of another race, there are issues that still loom large regarding stereotypes and political correctness about which you must be aware. You want to plan to avoid these landmines. Pay heed to those potential sensitivities and considerations as you prepare.

⇥ GAME PLAN EXECUTION ⇤

As the boycott emerged, I was asked if I could be available to go to Cuba to provide direct insight on the preparation for boxing. I could not believe anyone thought I even needed to be asked. How exciting would that be, sitting across the table from or at least being in the same room with Fidel Castro? In the end, I couldn't convince my boss to send me, and the decision was made to go with a small delegation. That was the end of my involvement, but I was to remain "available."

By all accounts, the negotiation was carried out to perfection, including mounds of specific information on the sports of boxing and baseball and the extensive security that would be afforded the Cuban delegation. When I asked Peter Ueberroth about the negotiation years later, there was still a spark of excitement in his voice, "You want to talk about my dealings with Fidel?" This from a man who went on to buy the Pebble Beach Golf course and serve as commissioner of Major League Baseball and chairman of the United States Olympic Committee.

Even with stellar execution, Ueberroth and the select delegation could not convince Castro to participate in the games. The effort included a solution that was designed to make Castro look creative. This was probably about plan C, D, or E in Ueberroth's preparation. "Send your baseball team only," Ueberroth suggested to Castro after plan A in the game plan—come to the games—had been delivered. Cuba then, as now, had some of the best baseball players in the world. Apart from any fears of defection, to send the baseball team alone, with its high probability of success in winning a gold or at least a silver medal, could be powerful.

Well, that didn't work. Overcoming the relationship and reliance that Cuba had on the still dominant Soviet Union was, apparently, insurmountable.

There was, however, one clear win for the organizing committee in the Cuban negotiation. This was plan F or G, but it was actually an integral part of the earlier possible deals. Ueberroth convinced Castro not to use his tremendous influence to discourage African nations from participating in the Olympics. This coupled with other efforts by the organizing committee led to the largest number of countries participating in the games up to that time.

In the end, there was a high level of satisfaction because all possible steps had been taken for us to have a shot at the best outcome. The preparation had been thorough.

Even if we didn't get the deal, we would at least want to feel that we gave ourselves the best opportunity to win. The only way to lose and walk away with your confidence intact is to know that you prepared thoroughly and with passion.

⇥ AGENDA SETTING ⇤

An important overlay to those negotiations was the establishment of a specific agenda. A key preamble to the actual substantive exchange in a negotiation of this type is to determine the order in which the issues will be covered. This strategy is key to ending up with the best possible outcome. An important part of planning any detailed negotiation is to establish the road map to get from the beginning of the negotiation to the end result that you desire. Your counterpart will, of course, want to establish an agenda that will drive the conversation in a direction most favorable to him or her.

An integral piece of this is usually a general agenda, but often a more specific agenda, setting forth the order in which specific topics will be covered, is determined as well.

This in itself can be a bit of a negotiation before you even get to the substantive issues. But it can also be a way to determine what each side views as the key issues that the negotiation must resolve. The amount of time that you will spend on this effort, or whether it will become an issue at all, will vary.

Of course, if all you are doing is establishing the price of a used car in a driveway, there won't be much of an agenda to establish. But if you are on the verge of negotiating a billion-dollar corporate merger, a negotiation agenda can be beneficial to both sides. I have had the occasion in my career to negotiate contracts for undrafted free-agent football players. The designated negotiator for the team and I both knew the relatively short drill of first, agreeing the player would go to that team and, second, determining the size of the bonus. The salary was known to be the then current minimum. We did not need an agenda.

On the other hand, when I negotiated the complex sale of a small sports agency concern to a larger one, not only did we have an initial agenda, we revisited the agenda over the yearlong process it took to close the deal. At times the agenda itself was the only detail we could agree on. The relative importance of the agenda will vary depending on the depth of the topic to be negotiated. The more complex the topic of negotiation, the more important the agenda.

⊰ CONTEMPLATING THE APPROACH ⊱

Another key piece of the preparation phase is determining if there are any steps you can take to move your position forward that will be viewed positively by the decision maker on the other side. For example, will your counterpart be more receptive to you if you act assertively? Or will that person be more receptive if you are casual and laid back? A negotiation conducted by Bob Johnson, the owner of the National Basketball Association (NBA) Charlotte Bobcats, provides some valuable insight on this level of preparation. The Johnson story illustrates the importance of knowing who the decision maker is. It also shows how you can give yourself the best chance to close the negotiation with a successful outcome.

In the Ueberroth example, there was no doubt that Castro was the ultimate decision maker. Not much research was needed to confirm that that was the case. But sometimes, the research step takes a long time, although the time spent is always well worth it.

In 2002, when Johnson was pursuing the opportunity to buy the then unnamed NBA franchise to be located in North Carolina, he could not have had a more formidable opponent to obtain the franchise rights: Larry Bird, the All World former Boston Celtic, the leader of a competing group that also wanted to win the expansion franchise.

Johnson knew he could not compete with Bird on the issue of who was more famous. He also knew that a price-bidding war was not going to be to anyone's advantage except the NBA owners. But even so, there were still a number of approaches Johnson could have taken to capture the rights. Johnson had made his fortune as the founder of Black Entertainment Television (BET). This is one angle he could have used. The NBA had no black owners, and many commentators argued that Johnson was the ideal pioneer. Johnson was rich, black, and media savvy, a combination that Bird could not compete with on any level.

Johnson had the opportunity to explore options, such as buying another NBA franchise, when BET was sold to Sumner Redstone's Viacom. Johnson earned billions as a result. Certainly Johnson had done a lot of research on the numbers, including the price tag for previous franchise sales. He understood these broad market reference points. But in this deal, the key question Johnson asked in his preparation was, *Who is the ultimate decision maker, and how do I proceed to convince him that I am the right buyer?* There were committees and owner cliques and individual powerful owners who at various times could be viewed as driving the transaction. But most people who know NBA business know that the commissioner, David Stern, makes most of the important decisions. Stern was Johnson's Castro.

This information was determined by careful conversations with those in the know. In those conversations Johnson sought out someone who could give him insight on how to deal with Stern in this situation. Here, just as with Ueberroth and Castro, winning the deal meant taking the time to determine how best to relate to the person across the table.

Johnson had a preexisting relationship with a longtime NBA owner, Jerry Colangelo of the Phoenix Suns franchise, who was close to David Stern. Colangelo's advice was simple: "Bob, continue to do whatever you are doing, keeping things low key, and continue to play the game. Talk to people and take your lead from us."

Johnson did. Throughout, he maintained a low profile and never unilaterally raised the race issue. That fall he was awarded the Charlotte franchise, which he later christened the Bobcats. A key reason Johnson won, especially over such a formidable opponent, was that during his preparation process, he learned not only who the key decision maker was but also the best way to deal with that person.

Your equivalent of Jerry Colangelo could be anyone from a former partner of whomever you are negotiating with, to a search engine like Google, which can provide a thorough background on the people you are meeting and the company they represent. In the end, you will have to gauge how reliable the information you have uncovered actually is and rely on it accordingly. The top tier of information is firsthand experience from or information about the past. The next level would be a Colangelo-type insider.

EXPERT TIP

Once you have analyzed your own position,
there is a person on the other side of the table
who is going to be really tough, and you have
to analyze his or her position as well.

—David Falk, Michael Jordan's longtime agent

⇥ Begin with the Basics ⇤

I grew up a baby boomer in Los Angeles, a kid possessed by sports, waiting for whatever game was coming up in whatever sport for whatever season. In the earliest years, it did not matter; I just wanted to play. In Southern California, for my generation, there were two coaches who had to have an impact on you if you had any thoughts of advancing to the next level in your chosen sport: John Wooden, the head basketball coach at UCLA and, for that brief amazingly teasing L.A. Rams moment, George Allen. Over the years, the one strand that ran through their successes, as well as those of others in and out of sports, was preparation.

I'll use the more famous of these men to make the point. The marquee name for preparation is John Wooden. We all should look to this man, who won a record 10 National Collegiate Athletic Association championships over the course of 12 seasons, to see what we can grasp from his success and see if any element is transferable to our business and personal life. His success has been featured in management and leadership books, but there is much from his leadership that is applicable to a top-level negotiating game plan. Here are some insights into his depth of preparation that are needed to successfully negotiate with the likes of Fidel Castro or David Stern.

"Gentlemen, today we're going to figure out how to put our shoes and socks on"—Wooden famously began each season with this instruction. "Socks," you say? Anyone can put on socks correctly before learning to tie shoes, right?

But Wooden knew that if the socks weren't put on properly, they would not fit snugly and there would be friction. That could lead to blisters, which could lead to a player not being able to play or, at a minimum, to personal discomfort. If the player happened to be a starter, or worse yet, a star like Lew Alcindor or Bill Walton, well, that truly could impact the outcome of the game, and ultimately even ruin a championship season.

Wooden wanted his players to roll up their socks and to carefully tighten their laces, instead of rushing through these motions in a hurried schoolyard manner. The wrinkles, especially at the toes and heels, had to be straightened out. At the beginning of the season, Wooden also checked on the players' shoe sizes to ensure that ill-fitting shoes did not lead to blisters because of all of the stopping and starting that players had to endure on the court. "I wanted it done consciously, not quickly or casually," he said. "Otherwise we would not be doing everything possible to *prepare* in the best way."

At the earliest stage, as planning for the task begins, the small details need to be addressed. That was an early step in Wooden's preparation, which began long before any game plan was even contemplated. Well, in many ways, this *was* a step in that ultimate game plan.

Wooden conveyed complete confidence in his team via his steadfast refusal to call a time-out in the final minutes of a game. No matter how close the score, he wanted the players to feel that they were fully prepared, that they were capable of winning, and that they therefore could execute the game plan at the highest level. This was Wooden's goal in this whole process. We should all prepare at this level.

Successful coaches like Wooden provide invaluable guidance on the importance of preparation and on the early steps you must take well before game time. Sure, this is about Wooden preparing for a game as opposed to a negotiation, but the psychology and the impact on the activity about to take place are exactly the same.

Preparation, as Wooden understood, can lead to flawless execution. With regard to Ueberroth's negotiation, a follow-up to Wooden's oft-quoted statement "failing to prepare is preparing to fail" resonates with us all. According to Wooden: "I believe there is nothing wrong with the other fellow being better than you are if you've prepared and are

Legendary UCLA basketball coach John Wooden

functioning in the way you've tried to prepare. That's all you can do."

Preparation puts you in the best possible position to win, whatever winning might be in a given setting. Castro was better positioned to not change his mind. In the case of the Bobcats, there was room for a win. You can only negotiate with the hand you are dealt, taking whatever steps you can to improve that hand and then using it to your advantage. The point conveyed by Wooden, too, is the importance of focusing on the basics.

David Falk, the longtime agent for basketball legend Michael Jordan, says: "Despite my longevity in the sports representation business, I always prepare thoroughly. I spend a considerable amount of time before every negotiation preparing, taking copious steps to understand the task I am about to approach." In spite of all his experience, Falk starts his preparation for each negotiation with a review of the most basic of documents, the collective bargaining agreement.

Sports lawyer W. David Cornwell, who represents star athletes and leading sports agents, puts in late nights reviewing relevant documents before every negotiation. The next day, even though he may not refer to any of them, he goes in confident and prepared.

⇒ FOCUS ON THE LITTLE THINGS ⇐

Chuck Noll, the four-time Super Bowl–winning football coach, once told his players, "Champions are champions not because they do anything extraordinary but because they do the ordinary things better than anyone else." This is certainly an extension of Wooden's preparation philosophy. You can't even do the ordinary if you don't take the time to master the basics. Master what you can do best.

Years before Super Bowl champion coach Tony Dungy heard those words from his pro coach, Chuck Noll, eerily similar words were delivered by his University of Minnesota college coach, Cal Stoll: "Success is uncommon and not to be enjoyed by the common man. I'm looking for uncommon people because we want to be successful, not average." There is a clear pattern about preparing and focusing on the little factors that is a constant theme with successful athletes. When Tony Dungy heard the words as a collegiate ballplayer, he knew that often we can overcome our lack of any uncommon traits with hard work (in negotiating it might be a vast vocabulary, photographic memory, or some other trick) by being uncommon in our efforts in preparing.

Dungy explains in his autobiography that "some players are uncommon because of their God-given natural abilities, like being blessed with the height of Yao Ming or the vertical jump of Michael Jordan. Others have to work to become uncommon. Steve Kerr of the Chicago Bulls shot five hundred free throws a day to make himself uncommon." We all have the basic capacity to be Steve Kerrs and Tony Dungys. We will enter the realm of the uncommon by virtue of our preparation. Will we take that uncommon step?

Where are we headed? You will learn what tools you have to prepare to a degree beyond all others and to reach the highest level of success. That is uncommon. In the broadest sense, all you'll be doing is understanding yourself better and preparing.

Simple? No, it's really hard and takes a lot of commitment and work.

Tony Dungy persuades teams to understand the importance of the *little things*—the importance of preparation with that level of focus. In his efforts to ensure that the team focuses on the minute factors, Dungy emphasizes the smallest of details and their execution; he gets his team to focus on his theory of "death by inches."

If you've ever seen the character played by Frank Sinatra at the end of the motion picture *Von Ryan's Express*, you're familiar with the theory. After quickly planning an escape from a World War II Nazi prison train, Sinatra chases a train commandeered by his prisoner colleagues with his hand extended to a fellow escapee who is reaching out to him, the last action that will get Sinatra to freedom and out of the rifle sights of the Nazis pursuing him on foot. Sinatra fails when he is shot and killed with his hand just inches away from the colleague. A little bit better focus on the plan to get back to the train and he would have been alive and successful. That's death by inches.

The greater the precision, the greater the likelihood of success. One mistake . . . well, you're not likely to die in a failed business negotiation, but you might wish that you had. That is what Dungy instills in his men: the precision needed to win a Super Bowl.

⇥ Establishing Credibility ⇤

One little thing to focus on is your credibility in the eyes of your counterpart. Credibility is important on two levels: your personal credibility and the credibility of the information you bring to the table. Even your counterpart will respect you more if you are credible.

It does not always have to be an overt statement of your pedigree, but if others don't know who you are or what your background is, there could be a gap that precludes the deal getting done. The early, get-to-know-you stages of a negotiation are a great time to establish your credibility, which could be based on your knowledge of the subject matter, your success record, or the people with whom you are associated. Establishing credibility is a small step that can pay dividends and lead to a more meaningful interaction. You should be much less shy about the credibility of your information. Be as specific as you can about the information you are sourcing. Ueberroth and Johnson didn't have to do much to convey their personal credibility, but most of us have to mount a focused effort in that department. Regarding the subject matter of their deals, both obviously had a bit more work to do. Ueberroth had to deal with issues such as the safety of the games, while Johnson had to deal with the price of previous franchise deals. Make a plan to assist the other side in believing your case.

⇥ Worst-Case Scenario ⇤

It is easy to prepare when you expect that all will go just as you anticipate, but how often have you prepared fully for the unexpected? You must be prepared for negative circumstances as well as for positive ones. Your counterpart may know that single piece of information you thought he lacked. He may actually have another option that you did not foresee. Spend some time thinking about that worst-case scenario and how you will respond to it. Most often this will be energy expended that you will never use. But how much more successful will you be if you are prepared the one time your counterpart says, "You have 10 minutes to make a decision or I'm moving on to the next buyer"? If you can go beyond a plan A and a plan B, complete the alphabet if circumstances allow. Hall of Fame coach Bill Walsh strived to be ready for every possible game situation "including the desperate ones at the end of a game when we may have only one chance to pull out a victory."

⇥ Create a Game Plan ⇤

What exactly do you want to plan? The rest of the book provides the specifics that expand upon the examples already mentioned. There are more steps beyond the broad basics that you've seen already, namely, knowing everything you can about the subject matter and the people involved; focusing on the cultural, gender, and race issues; focusing on the little things; establishing credibility; and contemplating the worst case. The template for a Negotiation Game Plan Worksheet follows. You have to view the template as just that—as a work in progress. It can certainly be used "off the shelf." You can make photocopies and pull one out each time you are preparing to negotiate. But like an offense that works well in a given sport, the basics are just the beginning. The playbook will be more successful for you if it is molded to match the personnel you actually have on hand. Most of us do not have the "ideal" that was envisioned, and tweaking the document to work for you will bring you even greater success.

⇥ TAKEAWAYS ⇤

Negotiation Game Plan Worksheet

1. My research tells me a range of possible outcomes, or *positive bargaining zone*, is:
2. My bargaining style is:
3. My counterpart's bargaining style is:
4. My credibility story about me:
   About my position:
5. The following cultural, racial, and/or gender issues will be important in this negotiation:
6. My desired agenda for this negotiation is:
7. My goal (a great outcome) in this negotiation is:
8. My walk-away point is:
9. A good outcome, my target is:

10. I do/do not plan to make the opening offer, but if I were to do so, my opening would be:

11. The role of relationship in this negotiation is:

12. The leverage in this negotiation favors:

13. My primary strategy is:

14. My plan B strategy is:

15. My plan C strategy is:

16. My plan D strategy is:

17. The ideal location is (restaurant, conference room with refreshments, via telephone):

18. Reference points that my counterpart is likely to use in the transaction are:

19. Questions that I will ask to seek information I need are:

20. My option if this negotiation fails is:

CHAPTER 2

STICK WITH *YOUR* STYLE

It's not how you play that matters—it's whether
you win; it's whether you're number one.

—George Allen, former Washington,
Redskins and Los Angeles Rams head coach

"I want you to come along with me as my lawyer." After
the exchange of a few niceties on the phone, this was
the initial request delivered to me. "I'm heading up the new
sports division for an entertainment management company." It sounded as though my former student had found
her dream job.

This was in the 1990s. The caller had been in my class
while a University of Pennsylvania student. You'll understand shortly why I am not disclosing any names.

Now she was a fledgling sports agent with a wealthy
financial backer and was preparing to visit a young man
who was a sure first-round draft football pick. Normally, I'd
have a much longer preamble with a potential client before

I got involved in a project. This time I broke my own rule. The professor in me thought that this could be fascinating, and I was also happy to assist a former student. I would soon realize that the negotiator in me should have thought about preparation; it was the old problem of the devil on one shoulder and angel on the other.

Two hours after getting off the phone, the former student picked me up at Penn, on the corner of 37th and Spruce Streets in front of the Wawa convenience store. She was driving a 1980 BMW 3 Series. I climbed in and slid the seat back as far as it would go, and in short order we were on our way to a housing project in Newark, New Jersey.

"Here, Professor, you might want to take a look at the contract." The former student reached over me into her glove compartment and handed me a letter-size manila envelope containing a document. For whatever reason, I didn't think a contract existed. I thought this was still the wooing period for potential clients. Maybe I was so surprised because the season was just ending and under National Collegiate Athletic Association (NCAA) rules, it was unlikely that an agent-athlete deal would be in place and signed. To remain eligible, a contract could not have been signed during the season just ended.

What had I gotten myself into?

Yes, this is partly an illustration of the negative impact of being unprepared and how easily we can fall into this sort of trap.

I undid the brass clasp. The envelope had not been sealed. I couldn't believe what I began to read. "Agency shall receive twelve percent (12%) of player's salary." This percentage far exceeded the maximum fee allowed sports agents by the relevant players' union. Something like 2 to 3 percent would have been more in line with the standards of the day. This was a freshly printed copy, and that, combined with my feeling about the season just ending, led me to continue to assume that this was a document still to be negotiated. I flipped to the end without reading the rest of it and was relieved to see that there were no signatures on it.

I can fill her in on the rules along the way, I thought to myself, still seeking to make the best of what was evolving into a bad situation. I figured that this was going to be a negotiation, and that's where I was going to come in handy.

"Oh, we have a signed copy, but no one knows about it," my former student told me after apparently seeing me rustle to the last page. She was trying to curb the anxiety that was coming over my face. Those words resonated in my head as the time flew by on the trip up the New Jersey Turnpike to Newark. What had I gotten myself into? The existence of a signed version of that contract made me very uncomfortable. The contract was so one-sided in favor of the new agency that I was confident that, even if not illegal, it certainly would not make it through the league's contract approval process.

At dusk, we pulled into the large parking lot of a well-maintained apartment building. It was then that the ultimate discomfort came over me. It was as though I were a character in a bad soap opera who wouldn't speak up, when saying just a simple "I didn't do it" would at least have saved my character's neck. When my former student and I walked into the apartment, I could feel the family's pride. During the introductions, it was clear that the athlete's brother was in charge. He was a fit, bespectacled young man in a starched white shirt with a dirty collar and thin tie. No more than 30 years old, he authoritatively instructed us. "Everybody come and sit at the dinner table," he said as he gestured toward a newly waxed four- by eight-foot-long oak table. "This is where we conduct all of our family's business."

I had a momentary vision of the kinds of conversations that must have taken place there with the two brothers and the mother. No father was present.

As soon as my former student, the athlete, his mother, his brother, and I sat down, the brother opened. "I want to congratulate you on writing the most fucked-up contract in the history of mankind," he said.

Wow, talk about a prison-punch opening. The term refers to the practice whereby if you are not a career criminal and you get locked up overnight for, say, drunk driving, you should immediately knock out someone in the holding tank. That will lessen the chances of your having any trouble in your brief overnight stay. Well, Big Brother wanted us to know that he had no intention of being taken advantage of by this Wharton duo. That was his style. If he had articulated it further in his language, he would have said: "I'm not up for any bullshit, and if you two clowns are anything like this piece of paper representing you, this meeting is going to be over in pretty short order."

He was looking out for his brother. And he was striking us first. He was using the style that he knew best, one that was comfortable to him and coincidentally was uncomfortable for us.*

⇥ KNOW YOUR STYLE ⇤

When NFL coach Bill Walsh installed the West Coast offense in San Francisco, he did not have a superstar quarterback. But he did have Steve DeBerg, a quarterback with adequate skills, especially in the short passing game. Walsh understood DeBerg's capabilities and molded the offense to those. That was, in fact, much of what prompted the design of the offense in the first place. When Walsh installed it at Stanford in the late 1970s, the first two quarterbacks in the system, Guy Benjamin and Steve Dils, had very different skill sets. The plays were but slightly tweaked to fit them. This was also the situation in the beginning with Virgil Carter as quarterback of the Cincinnati Bengals.

Beginning in the 1960s, negotiation and conflict resolution experts began lumping people into five categories:

---

* To use an example that has nothing to do with sports, when Luciano Pavarotti passed away in 2007, I was captivated by the conversation regarding why he was great—and I'm not a knowledgable fan of opera. Surprisingly, much of the commentary regarding his performing life centered not on how fantastic his voice or charisma was, but on his mastery of selecting works that were best suited to his style and capabilities. He was not trying to prove that he could sing in some unique range or display a variety of styles. All he was doing was what he did well.

avoider, competitor, collaborator, accommodator, and compromiser. The first time I heard about these categories of negotiating style, I thought back to people I'd seen negotiate, and tried to shoehorn them into one. I also thought of the coaches I had played for and how they used varying styles to influence the team to do what was in its best interest.

If you are a real chameleon, you can call on each of these styles at the appropriate moment, knowing when to turn one on, when to switch one off, when to move to another. But the majority of us do not have that ability. Just as with most things, there are probably one or two styles that are most comfortable for you. You should also know that multiple assessment instruments are available that enable you to get a professional read on who you are and what works for you. You can't control everything, but for those things that you can, put yourself in the best position to do so. Be prepared to adjust for those things you can't control.

Since knowing your negotiating style is such an important part of determining how to prepare for a negotiation, my colleague, Richard Shell, constructed a negotiation-focused Bargaining Styles Assessment Tool (BSAT) to help people better understand what works for them. *Before going any further,* I advise you to complete the assessment, which appears in the appendix. Once you have done it, return to this page; the text that follows will then assist you in getting a better feel for your bargaining style and what that means in the context of negotiating. The assessment will take you no more than 10 minutes.

For a basic understanding of what your scores mean, first make sure that you have accurately added up your totals and that they equal 30. Anything from 8 to 12 is high, from 4 to 7 is moderate, and from 0 to 3 is low.

The scores are about tendencies and comfort levels, not about absolutes, and you should view your scores accordingly. You are not locked into or out of any of the categories, but if you score high in one category relative to another, you have a better idea of where you are likely to gravitate. When you negotiate, the style that you will most likely use is your most comfortable default mode. The letters equal the tendencies set forth in the key below, and a basic description of each category follows.

As = Competitor   high
Bs = Collaborator mod
Cs = Compromiser   high
Ds = Avoider   low
Es = Accommodator high

Competitor (As)

"Competitor" is where most of us think we want to be on this scale. Whenever I administer this test, those who initially appear to be the happiest are the ones who have scored 10, 11, and especially 12 on competing. If you are reading this book, it is likely that you treasure the idea of being competitive. After all, it is the most competitive of us who succeed in sports. Most of us also believe that if we have a high level of competitive genes, we are likely to be more successful in the world of negotiating.

Unlike the avoider, a competitor loves to negotiate. Unfortunately, unlike the avoider, the competitor doesn't always know how to pick a battle and may too frequently be involved in disputes that are believed to be negotiations. Where the avoider might be more inclined to try subtler forms like persuasion and influence, the competitor has the tendency to enter full speed into negotiating.

When I think of the ultimate competitive personality, the tennis superstar Jimmy Connors best expresses those traits. Connors once said, "I hate to lose more than I like to win. I hate to see the happiness on their faces when they beat me." Connors and competitors love to win, no matter what they say, and they will go to extremes to do so.

If you score high on competing, you must ensure that a focus on relationships receives a prominent place in your game plan (this will be discussed later).

Collaborator (Bs)

For the more technically inclined of you who love puzzles, this may be your dominant trait. If you scored 8 to 12, there is probably not a riddle out there that you don't think you can solve, given enough time. You are not necessarily in a rush, and what you are seeking to do is put together the deal that others may not see. In doing so, you are looking to collaborate with the other side in order to assemble a deal that works for both of you.

It is clear that some of the best sports commissioners possess the collaborator trait. For example, the ability to call on collaboration skills is essential to bringing the National Football League (NFL) owners to agreement in the collective bargaining process in order to deal with labor. Owners are traditionally strong, independent individuals. The most graphic example of someone with this skill was the late Pete Rozelle, the commissioner of the NFL during its growth into the modern television era. He emboldened his team owners with what came to be known as "League Think" philosophy. He was able to make it clear to them that by working together they would be more successful than if they were constantly squabbling. Similarly, you can point to strong union leaders in sports having this same skill—the ability to bring together a broad range of players, from those earning the league minimum, to the superstars.

Compromiser (Cs)

Are you the one who always says, "Let's split the difference"? If you are someone who has the compromiser trait at a high level, that is likely to be one of your favorite negotiation ploys. If that statement is delivered at the appropriate time, it can work very well. Those who scored 8 to 12 on the compromiser trait probably are great at finding middle ground in their deals.

The problem comes when the difference is split at the wrong moment and the end result is not a number or outcome that ultimately makes sense for you. The biggest problem with this trait is pushing to split the difference even when that outcome will not get you to the right place. Compromise is powerful, but if used incorrectly, it can lead to some bad deals.

During one of our conversations, my colleague Shell told me the name of the person he most likes to use as an example of someone who clearly is *not* a compromiser. This person was at one time a fairly good boxer. He is a world leader, operating in an arena where compromise is often not the right answer. Splitting the difference is usually not the way to go. This strength was at the heart of the reason that he spent nearly three decades in prison. The outcomes he sought and continues to seek are the right outcomes, not a compromise simply to close the deal. That world leader and former boxer? Nelson Mandela.

Avoider (Ds)

The avoider category is related to the fact that negotiation is a form of conflict. Most of us would prefer not to be involved in conflict, so many of us have a pretty high dose of avoider within our personalities. If you are on the high end of the avoider scale, then you are cautious about entering into any negotiation; you'd prefer not to be involved in deal making. The most positive statement of your style is that you generally choose your negotiation battles very carefully. That is a very good thing.

Now, if you score low on avoid, you might want to evaluate whether or not you are too eager to get into conflict. You should focus on the possibility that you miss the opportunity to resolve matters before you enter into a full-scale dispute or negotiation. Might you better use some of the persuasion strategies in your repertoire before you go into high gear?

Accommodator (Es)

The high scorers in the accommodator category are likely to have an innate keen focus on the interests of the party sitting across the negotiating table. The high accommodator may even have a tendency to be overly concerned about the needs, hopes, and desires of the other side. This personality type, Professor Shell says, is like the concierge at the Four Seasons Hotel who, when you stand in his presence, constantly says, "How might I be of assistance to you?"

What the high accommodator needs to be most conscious of is that the other side is well informed on what his or her needs are. This person needs to be sure that there is a balance of information on the table that can lead to the best deal possible.

One place in sports where this style is seen with some frequency, surprisingly, is with sports agents—not necessarily in their negotiations with teams, but in their relationships with their player clients. In order to maintain their often tenuous client relationships, agents sometimes let the clients' well-being dominate their communications.

EXPERT TIP

KNOW YOUR STYLE AS WELL AS THE STYLE
OF YOUR NEGOTIATION COUNTERPART.

Competitor?
Collaborator?
Compromiser?
Avoider?
Accommodator?

The most common misconception is that in order to be a successful negotiator, you have to be competitive and forceful. The key point to remember is that no style is perfect for every situation. In fact, it's not the style at all, but rather the concept of doing the little things right over and over again, of avoiding death by inches by knowing yourself, of following your game plan, and of having a solid plan B (and even C and D) should you get diverted from that original path that leads to success.

⇥ USE YOUR STYLE ⇤

Back to my expedition sitting at that kitchen table in the apartment building with my former student. Following the powerful invective by the big brother, someone competitive might have tried to come back with an even more powerful zinger to the brother's telling us what he thought about the contract. I knew the worst thing to do would be to respond very competitively, especially if that was not the responder's natural style. At least I didn't make that mistake. I responded almost instinctively: "And I want to congratulate you on looking out for your brother's interests."

I'd gotten the sheepishness off of my face and was speaking calmly, all the while looking the brother squarely in the eye, with all sincerity. "I know the goal here is to see how we can make this work. So let's put this aside and talk about how these two young people, who have hit it off, can work together." The meeting was peaceful from then on. But I was anxious for it to end, to get back to my life as a professor, and to stay away from deals I did not put together.

In the end, despite the existence of the signed contract (which incidentally, I never did see—I steered clear of the whole relationship once I made it back to my office in Philadelphia), the player went with another agent. My impression was that the contract, signed or not, had rubbed the brother the wrong way. The brother called me in the midst of that negotiation process and asked if I had any interest in representing his brother. I thanked him, told him I was flattered, but said no. I'm sure you can understand why.

⇥ REVEL IN YOUR STYLE ⇤

The broad lesson that you should take from this chapter is to know who you are and who your opponent is in terms of style and, maybe more important, not to try to be someone you are not. Discover your strengths and base your preparation strategy on them. Be honest with yourself about what kind of negotiator you are, what you're good at, and what you are not so good at. If you are a stellar negotiator via e-mail, because of your avoiding and accommodating style, use e-mail. If you are competitive, try to sit across the table from your counterpart, especially if that person is an avoider.

Coach Walsh focused on the importance of being yourself and understanding styles, albeit for a different purpose. "Owners wanted someone who'd yell and scream and whip their players into submission," he said, "and I don't believe that's how to coach. I think you have to treat players intelligently." Walsh's heady style was not what we were used to seeing in the role of an NFL head coach, because that style is not usually what works in the coaching business. The style that works for the long run is the style with which the person is most comfortable. Walsh won four Super Bowls, the top prize in NFL coaching, and had a career record of 102-63-1.

The concept of sticking with your style applies to negotiating as well. How far can you go, how much can you accomplish, imitating someone else's style? What happens in the long, drawn-out negotiations when, in the end, fatigue will cause you to revert to the style that comes most naturally? It is easy to be yourself for the long haul; imitating another style is a formula for potential failure. Be yourself, and assert that style to the fullest.

Walsh's style was unique, and he knew it. But not all of us have taken inventory of who we are, particularly when

NFL Hall of Fame coach Bill Walsh

it comes to our own negotiating style. One of the fiercest defenders in the NFL participated in one of the Business Management and Entrepreneurship seminars we run for players at Wharton. These are men who have chosen to participate in our program, which helps them to transition out of the game and into their post-sports life.

The football–player student used the Bargaining Styles Assessment Tool, discussed earlier, and scored a zero on being a competitor. "How could that be?" he asked. Now, I did not want this guy mad at me, for all kinds of reasons, but I knew why he was angry. "Your bargaining style and playing style are two completely different animals," I told him. But he still wasn't very happy. Understandably, he knew in his mind what "competitive" was and felt that it described him. I told him to think about his playing position and how he knows what he can do best, whether it's using his strength versus using his speed or otherwise outsmarting his opponent. I pointed out that he knows when to call on which strength, and, as much as he may not want to admit it, he knows where his strengths lie and where he's not as strong. His style was that of a collaborative problem solver. As a leader on the field, that style was one he could ultimately accept and appreciate.

"You are not going to try and do something outside of that skill set unless you have to. You know how far off the ball you need to line up," I told the player. Now, you know that in business you may not be asking for enough—ask for more, push harder. Feel comfortable that that is okay.

This was actually an easy explanation for me to give to the player. I had once thought of myself as highly competitive in the negotiation setting. I think that most of us want to feel this way. The first time I did a formal assessment of my negotiation traits, I was pretty far along as a professional. I, like many, gave myself high marks in what I thought were the most important negotiation-style categories. I especially knew that I was competitive. I had been a competitive athlete all of my life, so certainly that translated into business as well. I had taken the Thomas-Killman instrument, a diagnostic test that measures aversion to conflict, much like Shell's Bargaining Styles Assessment Tool. The Thomas-Killman, too, is a good indicator of what kind of negotiator you are, at least in terms of the styles with which you are most comfortable. The results of my test revealed that I was not very competitive.

Around the time I took the test, I was in the middle of what had been an extended negotiation with a major firm that was seeking to acquire a smaller sports agency that I was representing. We were beginning to negotiate the numbers. My client and I had agreed, on this point, to go for a certain amount of money. With this new-found, less competitive image of myself, I decided to press for more. Even though I was a bit uncomfortable in doing so, I said, "You know, I took a test that said I'm not very competitive, so I'm going to ask for more than X; we want Y." My counterpart replied, "Sure, that sounds fair to me." My counterpart shocked me, didn't skip a beat, and then said, "Okay, what's the next issue we want to try to cover today?"

The important point here is, if you know your style and that asking for more, for example, does not come easily, there may be times where pushing yourself to the point of discomfort will bring you a better result. You don't want to thrust yourself fully into another negotiating style, but if there is a statement, a question, or an action that you can take that may improve your position, you should take that additional step.

For me, the additional step is the act of asking for more. For those who score low on accommodating, the additional step may just be a matter of asking more questions of your counterpart. Some people move to split the difference too often; others, not often enough. Understand the tendencies of your style. Learn to be flexible, but know that in the end you must stick with who you are.

⤚ SET THE ENVIRONMENT ⤙

As much as you can control it, you want the negotiation environment to be as favorable as possible to your style and your comfort level. Once you have a grasp of your style, you want to set the stage for the negotiation so that it is advantageous to you and detrimental to your counterpart. The tip that follows provides you with the key elements to think about.

EXPERT TIP

MESH LOGISTICAL DETAILS WITH YOUR STYLE

Agenda?

Location (yours, theirs, neutral?)

Via telephone, e-mail, in person,
or combination of these?

Number of participants?

Table shape and seating arrangements?

Ground rules?

Time allotted?

Refreshments?

Temperature?

There is little that is magical about your selection of any of these logistical details. The idea is to combine what is most comfortable for you with what will give you the best outcome in a specific negotiation.

"WIN" WITH YOUR STYLE

Bill Walsh suggested that you have to develop confidence in who you are, particularly as it relates to your style. Among the most famous NFL quarterbacks are Bart Starr and Johnny Unitas. Those two represent commanding, confident presences on the field. There was no doubt of their abilities and certainly no room for criticism by fellow teammates.

Then there is Eli Manning of the New York Giants, characterized by some as the deer-in-the-headlights quarterback. Manning does not display anywhere near the personality the world wants to see in a quarterback. He does not look confident in terms of tone and certainly not in terms of body language. But he does have a Super Bowl championship ring. The lesson that Manning provides is that the important thing is to accomplish the task at hand. In the National Football League the ultimate test, or goal, is to win the Super Bowl.

The epigraph by George Allen at the beginning of this chapter—"It's not how you play that matters—it's whether you win; it's whether you're number one"—gives us some guidance as to how we should view ourselves and others: not by style, but by whether we understand and have confidence in our style and, in the end, whether we can accomplish our desired outcomes.

Eli Manning has not become someone he is not. As much as people want him to be like his brother, the more outgoing yet serious quarterback Peyton Manning, or like one of the legendary football leaders, Eli seems to just keep doing what he is comfortable with. How unremarkable it should be that the simple act of knowing your own bargaining style can allow you to be the best that you can be. Know your style. As much as you can, learn the style of your negotiating counterpart. Use that information to prepare for your negotiation in an informed manner.

Here is one final style story that speaks to the importance of being yourself and true to your style: In an Indianapolis hotel room one day a somewhat exhausted person was interviewing multiple potential agents. The interviewer summoned the next interviewee: "Come on in, Mr. Parker." Into the room walked Eugene Parker, an attorney and sports agent. He was mild in presence, with little or no gravitas as he entered dressed like no one had been before him. The previous candidates wore a variety of outfits, with many close to the Superfly vintage of long-coated suits and floppy oversized felt hats, and even one fur coat. Parker's professional experience had primarily been at a traditional white-shoe law firm in Fort Wayne, Indiana. The story has it that his tie was a bit thin, shoes a bit squeaky, and pants a tad high-water.

After checking out Parker's appearance and talking with him for a few minutes, the interviewer exclaimed, "I'm sure you're not stealing anybody's money . . . you're hired." In an era when gold pinky rings, fur coats, and tailor-made clothes were more likely to be the style of the upstart agent, sticking with his own personal, more conservative style turned out to be the way to go. This was the meeting that won Parker one of the premier sports talents of all time. The interviewer was former pro football and baseball player Deion Sanders. By virtue of being true to his style, Parker landed one of the prize clients in professional sports. Certainly Parker's negotiation skills won Sanders over as well.

A key element in your negotiations is to know your own style and all that you can about your counterpart's style. Obviously, when you are dealing with your family, friends, and everyday coworkers, this is a simpler task than when you are going to negotiate with, for example, a leading agricultural official in Brazil. But that is part of the preparation that can lead to greater success.

⇥ TAKEAWAYS ⇤

1. Take the time to know your style.
2. Spend the time that it takes to learn the style of your counterpart.
3. Develop your strategy by fully incorporating your insight regarding the style of your counterpart.
4. Do not use a style that is not comfortable for you.
5. Do seek to make the logistics of the meeting favorable for you.
6. Be confident that you can be successful in negotiating against any style.

CHAPTER 3

SET GOALS AND AIM HIGH

I decided to set a $4 million floor for each potential sponsor.
Establishing a floor, or a minimum, is a negotiating
concept that has always worked for me.

—Peter Ueberroth, the most successful leader of a
modern Olympiad, wrote about his negotiating
goals for sponsors of the 1984 Olympic Games.

"You can be as arbitrary as you like and at the same time you see who dares to walk across the line." Ueberroth wrote this sentence following the 1984 Olympic Games. "This separates the serious businessmen from the phonies who want to take part in something just for the sake of it and from those looking for a cheap opportunity. It also forces bidders to think in terms of the numbers you want to deal with. In the end, if the winning bid is somewhere near your floor, the bidder feels he accomplished something—on his own terms." There is a strong correlation between the goals and the best opening offers.

The striking thing about this negotiation was that Ueberroth dramatically raised the floor, namely the minimum it costs a company to be an Olympic sponsor. Prior to these games the whole field of sports-related sponsorships was a mess, with a completely undervalued asset: the right to call yourself an Olympic sponsor. It is hard to understand now that there was little science to the pricing of sponsorships of any type prior to the 1984 Olympics. In the past, Olympic Games sponsorships had sold for relatively low amounts; the goal of the organizers was more about quantity than quality. The logic was that the more sponsorships that were brought in, the more money the Olympics would have.

But those numbers, with the largest in the tens of thousands of dollars, were actually in line with what the market called for. There was not much unique about being an Olympic sponsor. If you could come in with the same fee that the previous company paid, and there was no contract clause preventing your company from having an affiliation with the games, you could be a partner with the games too. In earlier Olympics there might have been three or four auto or soft drink manufacturers. There was nothing keeping your competitors from having the same designation that you had.

Before moving on to work with the Olympic boxing competition, I worked for the Los Angeles Organizing Committee in the sponsorship and licensing area. While pitching to potential sponsors, we would joke that past Olympic Games had had not only official domestic cars

Peter V. Ueberroth, chairman of the United States Olympic Committee, former commissioner of Major League Baseball, and president of the Los Angeles Olympic Organizing Committee

and official foreign cars but also official three-wheel and electric cars. Now we were offering exclusivity. The entire "automobile" or "gasoline" or "computer" category would be the sponsors', and they would not be sharing with anyone. And there would be only 30 official sponsors. Exclusivity combined with a hard ceiling on the numbers of sponsors and a hard floor on the minimum amount they would pay equaled the most profitable Olympics up until that time.

This thinking created an entire subsegment of the sports industry. Before the 1984 Olympic Games, there was virtually no sponsorship consulting expert. Now there are entire businesses guiding enterprises through the sports sponsorship terrain.

⇥ THE POWER OF GOALS ⇤

There is a psychology to getting successful negotiation results that is underused: visualizing the end result. Ironically, one of the best visualizers is basketball all-star Allen Iverson. He'll sit in a car on the way to a game and think through the moves he's going to make that evening. Visualization. The irony is that he is the one who famously protested, when reporters pressed him on missing a practice, "Practice, we're talking about practice, man."

Iverson is exceptional, but the concept of visualization is valuable for everybody. You are more likely to accomplish goals if you actually have them and then picture them in your mind. You are certainly more likely to achieve success if you have goals than if you don't have them. And with all due respect to Iverson, you probably have even a greater likelihood of accomplishing goals if you practice, or at least if you have some past experiences in achieving them. Many psychologists speak of this phenomenon as having "the power of expectations." The prevailing opinion is that you are more likely to accomplish those goals to which you have clearly and firmly committed.

When coaches put together their initial play list, their goal is for those plays to be successful. Coaches also employ one type of play to set up another. If things aren't working, or if there is a bigger advantage somewhere else, the best coaches can change plans midstream. But that flexibility needs to be balanced with the ability to make sure not to give up on the original game plan too early. You've got to have enough confidence in your plan to give it the fullest shot possible. Remember that Wooden philosophy, about planning and performing as well as you can, and not being overly focused on the opponent? Most of the success you will have in negotiating is not based on moves your counterpart makes but rather on how well prepared you are and how realistic your goals are.

The step Ueberroth took was the act of making the opening offer, something I have found people generally do not like to do. The big reason to consider making the opening? The powerful anchoring effect. But most of us prefer not to make the opening because either we don't want to reveal our position or we think we will gain some insight from what the other side has to say. Both reasons are valid, but the reality is, your comfort in opening increases in direct proportion to your comfort with the goal you have established. I'll discuss this topic more in Chapter 6. For now, keep in mind that your comfort with your goal is directly dependent on your level of preparation.

⇥ GOALS, TARGETS, AND ⇤ WALK-AWAY POINTS

In the Ueberroth example, his goal was to get $4 million from each sponsor. That was an ambitious number, but he put forth an argument about why, in those games, the value was so much higher than in the past. You should be of the frame of mind that achieving your *goal* is a great outcome. You can be flexible in the amount of ambition or optimism you feel about your number. Aim high (or low, depending on what side you are on). I view the goal as the highest (or lowest) position for which you have a credible story. If you can deliver your plea and it passes the chuckle test (that is, no one laughs out loud at the suggestion), that is probably your goal position.

You should also know your *walk-away point*. What is the minimum you will accept? You may have to delve into the negotiation a bit before you can put the numbers firmly in place, but your opening game plan should be as complete as possible. Be as firm as you can about your walk-away point as you enter the negotiation. The best way to determine your walk-away point is to focus on your options. I always ask myself and clients a key question: "What is my option if this negotiation fails?" That is actually the final query in the Negotiation Game Plan Worksheet (see Chapter 1). More formally, you'll hear this position referred to as the "best alternative to a negotiated agreement," or simply BATNA. If you have options that are identical to whatever you are negotiating, then the point at which you shut down is relatively clear. All other elements being equal, that point is when the price fails to fall a penny below your other opportunity.

A difficult walk-away point to determine is when you have no other options. In that case, it is more of a psychological determination of the point at which you think you could be comfortable with the outcome. The broader question you may be asking yourself is, "Can I live without this deal?" The clearer you can make that determination *prior* to entering into a negotiation, the better off you are going to be. However, if you need to make that determination *during* negotiations, you may want to take a break, assess any newly acquired information, and recalibrate your walk-away point. Never make such a decision under pressure.

Sports agent Tony Agnone stresses the importance of this: "There is nothing more powerful than for me to genuinely have the power to walk away if I can't get what I feel is right." Agnone goes on, "In my business this all revolves around proper preparation with a client."

EXPERT TIP

A stalemate is a great alternative to a bad deal.

— Arn Tellem, sports agent

The *target* requires a high level of precision. Where do you think this deal should close? What is the number, quantity, price, or whatever the metric is that you think, given the full impact of all of the information available, will close the deal fairly? This is the target. The bull's-eye.

Setting the appropriate goal, target, and walk-away points may be the toughest part of being a prepared negotiator. Keep in mind that you will not always be able to get all of the information you need to set all of these parameters with laserlike precision. This shortfall is what makes people most nervous about negotiating. It is this inevitable factual deficiency that should motivate you to gather as much information as you can before locking into these positions.

⇥ REFERENCE POINTS ⇤

Saying that you need to have a goal, target, and walk-away point is easy enough, but how should you establish goals? You do so with reference points, indicators that point you in the direction you want to go. An example of an ideal reference point, used in the automobile industry, is the

Kelley Blue Book, a manual referred to by car dealers and buyers to determine the price to set for used cars. It's the industry standard; it lists trade-in car values, dealer quotes, vehicle safety ratings—everything you need to know to establish a fair price. Is there something similar in your field? In your negotiations, your ideal counterpart would be this Mr. Kelley, who would supply the actual reference points that you could simply refer to during the talks.

Sports agents use reference points all the time; they love to point to a player on the same team as a client and say, "There is no way my client, with better statistics, should be paid less than that player." In other words, there is strength in saying, "I am basing my price on *your* standards. I did not just pull this number out of the sky. Isn't that reasonable? Are you prepared to call yourself unreasonable?" Psychologists, particularly Robert Cialdini in his bestselling book *Influence: The Psychology of Persuasion*, write about this human compulsion to be consistent and to appear reasonable. Make it your goal to combine a marketplace point of reference with references based on those actually used by your counterpart.

There are instances when there isn't much data on what the offer should be. How do you properly prepare in those instances? How do you avoid, for example, bidding too high? This often happens when there is an absence of reference points. The purchase of automobiles, again, although nerve-racking for many, is relatively easy because of the various guides like the previously mentioned *Kelley*

Blue Book and because of vast amounts of information on the Internet. But what happens when there is little information of that nature?

Japanese baseball players coming to the United States to play in Major League Baseball (MLB) give us examples of how an absence of reference points can create intriguing results. While playing in Japan, Ichiro Suzuki was known as one of the best baseball players in the world. His then team, the Orix BlueWave, clearly understood this. Suzuki's status was further amplified by U.S.-based agent Tony Attanasio. In 2000, Attanasio set up a simple blind-bidding process for Major League Baseball franchises to gain the right to negotiate with Suzuki. The Seattle Mariners won with a bid of $13,125,000. They outbid the next closest team, the New York Mets, by what was described as a substantial margin. In 2002, Suzuki became the first Japanese position player to play in the United States.

Where there are no clear market benchmarks, or reference points, we sometimes do see negotiators suffer from a bit of irrationality. This is especially the case in the bidding in free-agent athlete markets. With Daisuke Matsuzaka of the Boston Red Sox, it was structure as well as his extraordinary talent that allowed for the unique negotiations that took place in 2006. This was a magnified version of the 2000 Ichiro Suzuki negotiation. Matsuzaka was the star pitcher for his team in Japan, the Seibu Lions. The system for Japanese players to move to the United States has evolved into what is called a "posting." The first step, once the player is posted (made available for bidding by MLB teams) by the player's Japanese team, is for Major League Baseball to hold a sealed bid auction for the rights to negotiate with the player. The next step, once there is a winner of the bid, is to establish a period of time for the negotiations to occur. In Matsuzaka's case, the winner of this four-day sealed bid auction was awarded 30 days to negotiate exclusively with him. The Boston Red Sox won this right by bidding a refundable $51.1 million. Their league rival, the New York Yankees, had bid "only" $32 million.

The final step, once negotiations have been successful, is the right to negotiate a player salary. The final deal to sign Matsuzaka was for six years at $52 million. Once the auction took place and the money was in hand, the Seibu Lions wanted Matsuzaka to go. The $51.1 million fee the team received dwarfed its payroll that year, which was only $17 million. Keep in mind that this amount was what the Red Sox had to pay just for the right to negotiate a player salary with Matsuzaka, meaning they theoretically could end up with no deal. So knowing that his previous team would prefer not to have him back was a helpful bit of information. According to the Red Sox general manager, Theo Epstein, "We had strong indications that he [Matsuzaka] didn't want to go back to Japan and would be motivated to sign."

Matsuzaka's agent, Scott Boras, has the reputation of being one of the toughest negotiators in baseball. It was incumbent upon the Red Sox to put their knowledge of the negotiator aside and really focus on the information they had and the thorough preparation they had taken. According to reports, the initial offer by the Red Sox was to pay Matsuzaka a salary of between $7 million and $8 million per year. Boras reportedly was demanding twice that amount.

Now with the knowledge of the value the Red Sox placed on his client, Boras had a clear vision of how much the Red Sox were willing to pay. But in the end he had no real leverage; he was stuck, as is typically the case in team sports, with a single bidder. In the end the deal closed at close to the reported initial position of the Red Sox with a six-year $52 million contract. The total cost to the Red Sox ended up being $103.1 million.

So even in the absence of clear reference points, establishing a goal, a target, and a walk-away point is essential. If you don't develop these when preparing for a negotiation, you have a problem. It is important to understand the consequence of not having a goal or establishing one that is too low. Pat Summitt, one of the most successful coaches in the history of collegiate basketball, wrote, "Our goal every year is to win a title. You have to aim that high if you expect to reach a goal. If you expect to be No. 1, you might wind up No. 4. But if you just want to be somewhere in the top 10, you'll probably wind up a lot lower." So beyond setting a floor as Ueberroth did, it is also important to follow Iverson's practice of visualizing and thinking about how you are going to accomplish something. Set goals, not limits.

⇥ POWER OF COMMITMENT ⇤

You need to calculate your goal, target, and walk-away point with as much precision as possible. Your calculations will have a powerful impact not just on your bargain but also on you. In *Influence*, Cialdini opens the chapter on commitment with the reference to a study of people betting at a racetrack. The study finds that "just after placing a bet, they are much more confident of their horse's chances of winning than they are immediately before laying down that bet." So once you lock in on your goal, target, and walk-away point, it is hard to recalibrate. In the end, make sure you are ready to readjust after you have established those parameters.

"I'll tell you what we should do," I said. I was young and new at settling cases, but I knew what the target was. This was a libel case brought by an athlete, and I had sent a demand letter to the publisher. I demanded $100,000. This wasn't aggressive; it was really designed to leave some negotiating room, as we knew publishers typically did. It was a small matter, but we had done the calculation and it was worth, in the end, about $50,000. This was based on settlement numbers for similar cases.

I thought it was going to take some time, but this case was moving rapidly. We had sent the letter on a Wednesday, and here was the general counsel from the publisher calling me on Monday of the following week. He must have just received the letter. (This was well before the days that e-mail and Federal Express were widely in use.)

We exchanged some weather pleasantries, and then he went right into his plan. "Look, I've spoken with all of the parties on our side and we want to get this done."

Man, I thought, *this is going better than I ever could have anticipated*. "You're at 100, and I'll tell you now, we're at 50. I can tell you're reasonable. I'll tell you, I'm reasonable. I can't promise you anything, but what if I take this back to my side and tell them we've agreed to split the difference at 75?" Not only was he shortcutting the negotiation, but he was also leaving three zeroes off the numbers. I confirmed, "You are offering $75,000, correct?" He did not hesitate, "Yes, if we can settle this matter today."

My instant impression of Mr. General Counsel was that no one could be more reasonable. Apart from my impression of him, he had rolled the dice a bit too. He was betting that I was a compromiser. Someone competitive would see the opening and go for more, right number or not. The problem solver might recalculate, but in the end probably go along with the deal. The avoider, to some degree, would be in the right frame of mind to strike a deal with me: "If I have to negotiate at all, I want to make it brief." Well, I don't know what my exact words were in response to the offer, but he convinced me on two points: first, my target was met and surpassed; second, he had suggested a fair compromise. I took it back to my client, and I didn't suggest that we ask for more. I should have. At this stage of my thinking about negotiating, I did not maintain a separate target and goal. I combined the numbers and really gave myself little room to stretch, to have a truly superior outcome.

It was years later, when I formally began to study negotiations, that I realized I had been part of a textbook case. But back then I didn't know myself and my own negotiating style. Nor did I know this negotiation strategy. I now use it, and you should too, particularly if you know the person across the table from you is a compromiser.

I should have taken a break and regrouped. This was an instance where no action on my part was necessary other than making the simple statement "I'll take your offer under advisement." I was not listening carefully enough, not patient enough, and too anxious to close. I was too committed to the numbers I had established before the negotiation got underway. We settled at his offer of $75,000. Not a bad deal, but one that had the possibility of being even better.

⇥ REALISTIC GOALS ⇤

We can also get in trouble by being too ambitious with our goals. The collective bargaining process between the National Hockey League (NHL) and the National Hockey League Players Association (NHLPA) provides us with one final example on the importance of establishing viable targets, goals, and walk-away points. League versus union discussion over the collective bargaining agreement in hockey, as well as in other professional unionized sports, is the negotiation that determines all of the important issues between the league's management and the players.

This was 2004, and the hard initial line that the union was basing its stance on was no salary cap in any form. Salary caps are a form of spending control for a given league's owners. Basically what the cap does is limit what a team can spend on player salaries. In terms of financial and fan interest, hockey was hanging on by only a thread as the fourth of the major four sports in the United States.

The telling conclusion of this negotiation is that the deal the union ended up with could have been accepted when it was offered at the very beginning of a long, drawn-out public negotiation. Remember, preparation is where the real work comes in. Movies, television shows, and newspaper and magazine articles are always about the exchanges, the old smoke-filled rooms, and the final late-night meetings. What they don't reveal is what went on before—the preparation. But without that vital step, the upper hand would never be gained by either side.

The NHL locked out its players on September 15, 2004. This longtime labor strategy, a lockout, allows management to control the timing of a business shutdown, rather than being surprised by a strike. After five months of canceling games, the league made the painful decision to end the season.

Many events led up to the lockout. First, the league could not land a traditional big-four sports league television contract. The other key issues were the losing financial seasons suffered by 19 of the 34 franchises and the total league losses of $225 million the previous season. This prompted the league to seek to reduce the average player salary from $1.8 to $1.3 million.

The issue that the union and the league had most difficulty agreeing on was the implementation of a salary cap on the total percentage of league revenues that could be used to pay player salaries. The owners' offer was at $42.5 million, and the union was at $49 million. As close as these numbers seemed, and even though this stalemate was reached as the parties inched forward, they could not finalize a deal. As a result of the lockout, over half of the NHL players left to play for teams in Europe.

The NHL and NHLPA then had a public relations nightmare on their hands. After the players were locked out for 310 days, the final starting deal was reached. The players agreed to a salary cap of $39 million per team. That's right, this was July and the players were accepting a deal that gave them $3 million less than they had been offered in February. How could this happen? This was the perfect storm of miscalculating one's position, the lack of leverage, and the fortitude of one's counterpart. The NHLPA did not "play smart." The relevant negotiating numbers needed to be contemplated with all of the available relevant factors. Coach Pat Summitt urges us to aim high, but these lofty ambitions must be tempered by reality.

In your planning, you must develop aspirational goals, realistic targets, and clear walk-away points. You should also have some flexibility depending on information you gain during the course of a negotiation.

❧ Takeaways ❧

1. Do the appropriate preparation to establish a target, goal, and walk-away point.
2. Use your counterpart's reference points.
3. Set goals high.
4. Be realistic about targets; put the stretch in your goal.
5. Be firm about your bottom line, absent new data turning up in the negotiation.
6. Revise targets and goals cautiously as you get new data.

CHAPTER 4

SEEK LEVERAGE

This is for Rudy.

—What player after player said in the motion
picture *Rudy* as they gave Notre Dame head
football coach Dan Devine their jerseys indicating
they would not play against Georgia Tech unless
Rudy was allowed to play.

"I'll pay you $5 million" must have been the words Don
King uttered. As a newcomer to boxing, there was
no way for him to become a big-time player in the boxing
game without a truly unique offer. In the end, King struck
one of the landmark deals in sports.

King managed to convince Muhammad Ali and George
Foreman to fight each other, based on King's promise of a
record-breaking fee and his word that the other pieces were
coming together. The two men signed separate contracts
stipulating that the money was not payable immediately,
so King had time. He moved swiftly. King had to find

someone to actually put up the purse, because he personally did not have that kind of money.

To make that happen, he told the leader of a developing country, "If you'll pay the cost, I'll deliver you the heavyweight title bout." This was intriguing. Up until this time, championship bouts were limited to high-profile cities, such as Paris, London, and New York.

Ali had been banned from boxing for three years as a result of his antidraft stance on the Vietnam War. Amazingly, he had battled his way back from being stripped of his title in 1967, the crescendo being the January 1974 defeat of Joe Frazier in a unanimous 12-round decision in New York City's Madison Square Garden. He was still not the old Ali, but that victory made it clear that he was a force to be reckoned with in the heavyweight boxing ranks.

At the time, the heavyweight champion of the world was George Foreman. In order to retain that title, before the Ali-Frazier fight, Foreman knocked Frazier out of the ring in their earlier championship bout in Kingston, Jamaica. That knockdown, the one that prompted the broadcaster Howard Cosell to deliriously repeat in an epic rhythm, "Down goes Frazier! Down goes Frazier," was one of the most powerful blows ever delivered in heavyweight boxing.

With Frazier as the losing lynchpin in those two bouts, every promoter in boxing wanted to have the Ali-Foreman fight in his catalogue. The paradox was that none of the promoters of the day—Bob Arum, Jerry Perenchio, or even Madison Square Garden's Teddy Brenner—had the inside track.

As one commentator appropriately said regarding King putting this fight together, "This was the opportunity of a lifetime for Don King. He put everything into it—all his will, all his energy, all his showmanship, all his mastery of numbers, all his skill at preaching an evangelical paradise in the future to black brothers." Even with all of this, what King really demonstrated was that he understood leverage and how to negotiate.

The cost was the $5 million he promised the boxers and the expense of putting on a bout in Zaire. The leader was Mobutu Sese Seko of what was, in 1974, Kinshasa, Zaire. The bout took place on October 30, 1974.

King positively leveraged the parties and the entire deal by making both sides, really multiple sides, believe that he could put the whole package together. This Don King theory of transitivity—the "if this, then" kind of view—is often the key to bargaining.

There is a lot of persuading that has to go on to make this type of deal happen. With Ali, there was the added requirement to make periodic payments over time leading up to the fight. The deal stipulated that if King missed a single payment along the way, Ali was released from the deal and kept all of the money paid up until that time. That too, obviously, served as an additional incentive for Ali to enter into a deal with this unproven promoter. King made those deadlines.

King's leverage was powerful because he was perceived to be the one, the only one, who had what the parties wanted, even if, as in the case of Mobutu, they did not know that's what they wanted. King connected with the interests of all of the parties to make the deal happen.

In the case of Mobutu, King understood the leader's ego and how he wanted to be a star on the global stage. Mobutu's vehicle would be the World Heavyweight Championship bout. This was the bout that King would christen "The Rumble in the Jungle." No one else had ever presented anything like this to Mobutu, just as no one else had offered either boxer as much money. It was a subtle form of leverage—if you don't deal with me, you won't get this—and a unique one, because the deal maker created the leverage from sources he did not control. King's promotion provided the vehicle for Ali to knock out Foreman and regain his title.

⊰ FINDING LEVERAGE ⊱

The number-one question I have received over the years is, what can I do if I don't have leverage? Everybody wants it, but it's not always there. Regarding leverage, the lesson from Don King is this: work hard to create it. It is a delicate dance to create leverage in the way that King did, since initially he had so little in hand.

I was involved in a few boxing negotiations with King. I recall one in particular where my side had very little, or probably zero, leverage. That being the case, I advised my

Boxing promoter Don King

client to ultimately take the deal King offered. For King, this probably was just another boxing deal. For me, this was an opportunity to incorporate into my preparation the formidable reputation of Don King.

My client was the 1984 Olympic heavyweight gold medal winner, Henry Tillman. The last correspondence I received from Tillman came hundreds of deals and millions of dollars after the Ali-Foreman bout. "King is threatening to cancel if he does not have this closed in an hour," Tillman wrote. My thought was that we had to look at the offer from King's perspective. It was very easy for him to move on to another boxer who would be happy to take even less. King needed an opponent for his boxer. Tillman was a bit of a risk as an opponent, and maybe King had not fully focused on that. At some point, you really know the offer on the table is the last one.

A most unlikely sporting event took place that made this deal a possibility. Mike Tyson was the surprise knock-out victim in the heavyweight championship bout in Tokyo on February 11, 1990. The winner was Buster Douglas, and it was at 42–1 odds, the biggest upset in boxing history. Prior to their bout, all believed Tyson to be invincible. His record was then 37 and 0, with most of his fights ending in early-round knockouts.

Following that Tyson loss to Douglas, Tyson's promoter, King, needed a comeback fight for Tyson. Someone who had credibility so that Tyson could get back into the game. Tillman was a great candidate because he had beaten Tyson twice in 1983, when they were both amateurs competing for the slot to represent the United States at the Olympic Games at the heavyweight level. This is what made Tillman a remote risk. Every great heavyweight boxer, except for the undefeated Rocky Marciano, always seems to have at least one opponent who has his number and who knows how to beat him. Could Tillman be to Mike Tyson as Ken Norton was to Muhammad Ali, for example?

"Henry, I have an opportunity for you that I hope you are interested in." It was Don King calling Tillman at Tillman's home in Diamond Bar, California. The initial offer was strikingly low—one-third of what we anticipated Tyson was going to receive.

It was a large amount of money. But when you know your opponent is being paid three times as much as you, you might believe there is some bargaining room.

King entertained some back and forth, and then delivered the message, saying essentially, "If you don't sign in an hour, I'm going on to the next boxer." At some point you've got to be aware of when you've exhausted whatever leverage you have. Sure, there was no one else who had beaten Tyson, but there were others with bigger names who could be promoted just as successfully. At this moment it was clear that King was through and Tillman had to make the decision: take this or miss out on the payday and the tremendous opportunity. He signed, and Tyson won the fight by a first-round knockout.

⊰ COALITION BUILDING ⊱

My motion picture imagery of leverage comes from *Rudy*, the story of Daniel "Rudy" Ruettiger and his improbable pursuit to play football at Notre Dame. This is the feel-good story about a blue-collar kid determined to become a football hero. In the movie, the climax comes as Rudy is about to close out his career without having played in a game for even one minute. In spite of that, he's already had more success than he possibly could have imagined, for he made the Notre Dame football team as an undersized walk-on. The motion picture emphasizes that no one thought Rudy would be admitted to Notre Dame in the first place, let alone make the football team as a player the school did not recruit. Nevertheless, in a unique way, Rudy has become an integral part of the football team. This is clearly the head coach's viewpoint, but he is not about to put Rudy on the field.

The scene, though, is another great example of leverage coming seemingly from out of nowhere. Starting with the star players, the members of the team come to Coach Dan Devine's office and say their own versions of "this is for Rudy" as they place their game jerseys on his desk, indicating that they want Rudy to play in their stead. The coach might be able to push back on one player, but following the leader of the team, player after player walks in and we are shown the coach's face clearly expressing "I've got to let Rudy play." The players created leverage by building a coalition.

Orchestrating leverage is a unique skill. Devine's players illustrated that it wasn't necessary to be heavy handed. It didn't take a player's strike or a vocal confrontation during a team meeting, but rather a subtle expression of desire and a clear message to the coach that said, "Look, you may have had the upper hand, but by forming this coalition we have shifted the leverage to our side now." It is the overbearing use of leverage that can provoke an irrational response from the other side . . . or one that might seem irrational that actually works.

≫ FAULTY COALITIONS ≪

The National Hockey League Players Association (NHLPA) discussion in Chapter 3 was an example of an unsuccessful coalition—largely due to the absence of leverage. Dan Devine both needed and believed the members of the player coalition. The players there used a single game. It gets more problematic when there is an attempt to hold a coalition together for a longer period of time. The use of replacement players in the 1987 NFL players' union strike gives us some insight into this. In that situation, the NFL players were striking for greater benefits and earnings, among other issues. The ultimate thought by players in any sport is that there is no way they can be replaced due to their unique skill level. Not only did the owners field teams that featured unknown replacements, but that move also prompted some veteran players to cross the picket lines.

The leverage of the National Football League Players Association (NFLPA) and NHLPA players was not what they thought it was. These players are not alone. Overvaluing leverage or power sometimes occurs. It is important not to flaunt power when you have it or perceive that you do. And this is true not just because circumstances might change, but also because you may have misjudged your power or, even more surprisingly, your counterpart might prefer walking away or doing a different, even inferior, deal simply because he would prefer not to be associated with you.

The cricket business provides further interesting insight. The Indian Premier League (IPL) was formed in 2007 with eight franchises gearing up to play a 56-game season. The fans were excited, and the advertising dollars made the league an almost instantly valuable enterprise.

One of the steps that league officials took was to restrict the publishing of Internet reports and photographs, at least if the financial dividends did not flow to the IPL. The IPL also refused to accredit Web sites to telecast the games. Further, the IPL wanted to retain sole copyright of the images. Photographers were required to upload photographs to the official IPL site within 24 hours of taking them.

The media responded by forming a coalition. With that newfound power, Reuters and the Associated Press threatened to boycott the IPL matches. As a result, the IPL removed its restrictions on newspapers and Web sites using the photos. The Fédération Internationale de Football Association (FIFA) had tried a similar move in the 2006 World Cup, and that attempt failed as well. That was a lesson the IPL, with thorough preparation, could have learned a lot from.

⊰ Lying ⊱

My view is that when establishing leverage, honesty is essential. This dictum generally becomes an issue for people when they perceive that they don't have leverage and they begin to seek ways to create it. We were confident that King was not bluffing and that he could easily go on and offer the same contract, or even a lesser one, to the next boxer. King had, in negotiation-specific jargon, the best BATNA (again, the best alternative to a negotiated agreement). That proved to be especially true when King, in his promotion of the fight, did not aggressively use the fact that, as amateurs, Tillman had beaten Tyson. It was clear that any good boxer could have filled the role. It was clear that King had to know that we had no BATNA other than Henry Tillman going back to studying for the real estate broker's exam. The party with the best BATNA has the best leverage and is likely to get the best end of the deal. It is the absence of a strong BATNA that probably most often leads to lying.

Anyone can have success with a single deceitful act—maybe even several successes. But once the word is out, once your credibility is damaged, it is nearly impossible to get it back.

Jeff Moorad, now the president of the Arizona Diamondbacks, was a onetime agent. Regarding one fellow agent known for his dishonesty, Moorad said, "I don't think there is a general manager in baseball that believes him when he says he has other teams interested. He is known to misrepresent the facts."

Football agent Leigh Steinberg writes about the importance of leverage from his perspective. His primary focus is on ensuring that the other side thinks he has a competing offer. He actually incorporates this into one of his 12 essential rules: convince the other side that you have an option.

You can certainly focus on making the other side believe you have an offer, but it can become a slippery slope. It is an easy lie to fall into. I caution you: in your preparation, develop your game plan regarding competing offers carefully. But, of course, if you lie and get away with it, you may have substantially improved your position, unless your lie is uncovered.

I asked Jared Bartie, a team executive with the Charlotte Bobcats, "What is the most important negotiating tip you could convey?" The answer? "Maintain your integrity. You don't want to get a negative reputation in the business. Stay true to your word."

EXPERT TIP

A gold medal is a wonderful thing, but if you're not enough without it, you'll never be enough with it.

—Irv Blitzer (John Candy) *Cool Runnings*

Like many industries, sports, with thousands of participants, in the end turns out to be pretty small. Similarly, it gets even smaller if there is negative information flying around about you.

As do many of the issues, this all goes back to preparation. You are most likely to remain truthful throughout if the message you deliver is one that was planned rather than one that was made up spontaneously to protect your best interests.

Most of us prefer to be honest in negotiations. The first step is to make the personal commitment to be so. Then, many of the answers to difficult questions become a lot easier. For example, if you are planning a splashy event for a company launch, you may be charged with hiring a public relations firm. You tell the representative you are thinking about having an opening gala. The representative, prior to your agreement to engage her, may say, "Sure, we'd love to work with you on this. What's your budget?" Now that you are in the negotiating mode, your first thought would be, *if I give her a number, she will use that to determine her fee.* So rather than lowball what your budget is, you might say, trying to gain a negotiating advantage on fee, "Well, let's discuss your standard fees first." This is another way of saying, "We are in the midst of a negotiation here. Why would I want to show you all of my cards?"

⇥ Exercising Leverage ⇤

In addition to the Don King example, the successful use of leverage is also illustrated by two National Football League (NFL) quarterbacks, John Elway and Eli Manning (see Chapter 3). Each was potentially the first pick in his respective draft—Elway in 1983 and Manning in 2004.

Elway was determined not to play for the Baltimore Colts. He had leverage; he had already signed with and played for the New York Yankees baseball organization the two previous summers. He was drafted by them in 1981, and although he batted .318, views were mixed on whether he could make the big leagues. With George Steinbrenner at the helm of the Yankees, all knew there could be stiff monetary competition, if that was truly what Elway wanted to do.

He was not given his choice, at least not right away. Despite Elway's expressed desire to play on the West Coast, Baltimore stubbornly did not trade the pick to San Diego, Seattle, or Los Angeles. "I don't want to be a jerk or anything," Elway told then Colts coach Frank Kush, "but we ["we" meant Elway, his agent Marvin Demoff, and his father, Jack, the then head football coach at San Jose State] have been telling you for three months, I'm not going to play in Baltimore." Elway then called a press conference to declare, "Right now, it looks like I'll be playing baseball with the Yankees. [The Colts] knew I held a straight flush and still they called me on it." In the end the Colts traded Elway to the Denver Broncos, where he signed a six-year contract for $12.7 million.

Eli Manning's leverage was less evident. He did not have the baseball alternative. He just made it clear that he did not want to play for San Diego. The Manning family reportedly said that playing for the Chargers was not conducive to their son's future. The San Diego Chargers finished the 2003 season with a 4–12 record, which was the worst record of any team in the NFL that season. This entitled the team to receive the first overall selection in that year's draft. The Giants also finished 4–12 and decided that the team's primary need was a franchise quarterback. Manning's leverage? It was that he might not play. More important, the Chargers did not need a protracted negotiation and saw a way to avoid that—give in to Manning's desires.

There was some irony here. Ernie Acorsi, the general manager of the Giants, had also served as the general manager of the Baltimore Colts when the team lost Elway. This time Acorsi was playing the role of spoiler, and he saw Manning as a talent similar to Elway. The Giants used the fourth overall pick to select Philip Rivers, whom the team then sent to San Diego along with the third-round pick and the first- and fifth-round picks in the next year's draft, in exchange for Manning.

⇥ INCREASING LEVERAGE ⇤

In 1966, two of the greatest pitchers ever to play on the same team at the same time were Don Drysdale and Sandy

Koufax. This was in an era when there was not much leverage on the part of players because there was little chance of them moving to another team absent a trade; there was no free agency. Agents were not yet in common use. The two Los Angeles Dodgers pitchers hired a Hollywood movie producer, J. William Hayes, to negotiate their deal, and he had a vision of leverage that had not yet been exercised; he threatened to hold both of them out unless the Dodgers met his salary demand of $167,000 per year for each player for three years, the first $1 million holdout in sports. This annual figure was $47,000 more than the salary of the highest-paid player of the day, Hall of Famer Willie Mays. In the next round of collective bargaining, Major League Baseball moved to bar collusion of this type by players. The union agreed, provided the teams agreed not to collude as well.

So whether through belief in your skills or persuasion, like Don King, or by other forms of creativity in putting together leverage, like producer J. William Hayes, leverage is invaluable.

⇥ LEVERAGE VIA TIMING ⇤

There are two issues related to timing and leverage that are important. The first is that leverage is fleeting. Circumstances can change, and you can lose it. The other timing issue is how the parties view the future value of a deal. This is a fleeting concept too, but it comes up frequently in sports when the endorsement value of an unproven athlete needs to be determined. Consider the high school or college player moving up the ranks.

If you don't act on leverage quickly, it may be gone. In some transactions, this means that the high price you may have been offered is no longer available. A good example of shifting leverage is the signing of the soccer player Ronaldo by the Italian professional soccer club AC Milan in 2007. Originally the club was willing to pay a transfer fee of $28.5 million to Real Madrid, the team Ronaldo was playing with at the time. But after a few months, AC Milan was able to get him for only $9.73 million. Timing. AC Milan's level of interest declined. The message is that leverage is often fleeting. You need to move on it while you have it.

Timing certainly works best when you have leverage. But sometimes placing artificial time constraints can bring a deal to closure as well. "If we don't resolve this today, we won't discuss it with you again until the season is over." Agent Stanley King threw this at management regarding one of his star baseball clients. He had permission to say it, so it was not idle. This gave him the ability to deliver the statement with confidence. The next thing King knew, "We were locked up in a conference room until 11:00 p.m. We got it done."

Anna Kournikova was astoundingly successful in gaining endorsement opportunities without initial professional success on the tennis court. So far the same has been

Young golf phenom Michelle Wie

true of golfer Michelle Wie. Similarly, basketball player LeBron James was financially successful in the endorsement world before he proved himself in the NBA; he signed an initial astonishing $90 million deal with Nike.

Nike and the other endorsers of these athletes are similar to investors seeking to participate early in a new business venture. If the proposal looks strong in all ways, everyone believes there is value to getting in on the ground floor, while it's least expensive. The seller has the task of being even more persuasive about how great the idea will perform, beyond the perceived expectations.

This was the case with all three of these athletes. Kournikova, for example, had not only world-class tennis talent but also striking good looks. That was the edge that she had over comparably talented athletes. That is what Kournikova and her representatives were able to use to gain endorsements, to the tune of over $15 million per year, without her ever achieving the highest level of play.

Similarly Michelle Wie is a young golfing phenomenon. She too is an attractive young woman and, like Tiger Woods, is enjoying success in golf at a very early age. Sponsors were fearful of missing out on the opportunity to be associated with a female Tiger Woods. The thinking by companies was, if we don't sign her up, maybe others will freeze us out of the opportunity. As a result, she signed deals valued at over $10 million in her first year.

Phil de Picciotto, a veteran negotiator and the president of Octagon Athletes & Personalities, calls these "futures" negotiations. He suggests that when you are in these situations, you carefully tune in to the emotions that are driving the other side. Asks de Picciotto: "Why are they potentially interested? How deep does the emotion run and how can I capitalize on that?" The key is to assign value to that emotional assessment.

⇥ LEVERAGE FROM CONSISTENCY ⇤

Leverage is often supported, too, by the element of consistency, which was discussed in Chapter 3. People want the same standard applied to them that was applied to others. People want to be perceived as being reasonable and want to act consistently for that reason. This is especially the case where there is public information on similar previous deals.

"Al should just say, 'Gentlemen, I'll take the Rosenbloom deal.'" So said Al Davis's lawyer and the former mayor of San Francisco, Joe Alioto, at an NFL owners meeting focused on the proposed relocation of Davis's franchise, the Oakland Raiders, to Los Angeles. In Davis and Alioto's view, the owner of the Los Angeles Rams, Carroll Rosenbloom, had not sought league permission when the Rams uprooted themselves from Los Angeles to Anaheim, 50 miles south. They also did not pay any sort of fee for the privilege of moving to an as yet undeveloped NFL territory. Rosenbloom simply entered into an agreement with the city of Anaheim to move his franchise, and four months later the owners approved the move.

At the heart of this distinction was Rosenbloom's long-time positive relationship with his fellow owners, compared with the often cantankerous and rebellious presence of Davis. It was Davis, after all, who had once headed the rival American Football League, which had battled with the NFL throughout the mid-1960s. All was not easily forgotten, even the fact that Pete Rozelle, and not Davis, had been named the commissioner of the merged leagues. The bad blood ran both ways.

The agenda at this meeting in the early 1980s was focused on figuring out what it would take for Davis to relocate his Raiders to Los Angeles from Oakland. He saw much greener pastures in the huge, open Los Angeles market than he had in the San Francisco Bay Area market he was then sharing with the 49ers. But Davis had done nothing to endear himself to his fellow owners. His actions were completely counter to the prevailing "League Think" philosophy that then Commissioner Pete Rozelle had instilled in the franchise owners.

Davis, as irritating as he was to the league, just wanted to be treated consistently. That consistency assertion, and the leverage Davis thought it would provide, was not enough. The NFL owners did not vote to give Davis permission to relocate. The negative relationship between Davis and the league appears to have trumped the power of leverage often gained from the consistency principle. As a result, litigation ensued.

In the end, the best leverage is powerful because it is known to the other side to be both sincere and executable. Coach Devine knew players were at the point where they were willing to risk not playing themselves if Rudy did not play for Notre Dame. Elway was going to play baseball. The toughest negotiations are the ones where you have little or no leverage relative to your counterpart. In many ways, leverage can be developed if you are able to create a positive, credible vision of the future. Establishing that is not always easy, but that is the task when you have little else in hand. Leverage can be found with coalitions, with timing, through consistency, and by properly using the relevant reference points. But no matter how much leverage you have, the existence of a negative relationship may prevent you from closing your deal. We'll explore this relationship issue further in the next chapter.

⇥ Takeaways ⇤

1. Look under every stone for leverage.
   Orchestrate powerful leverage where you can.
2. Be sincere if you lack leverage.
3. Do not flaunt leverage.
4. Use leverage quickly; its use may be fleeting.
5. Be aware that the most powerful leverage may be
   the reference points established by the other side.
6. Understand that a negative relationship
   may trump the power of leverage.

CHAPTER 5

FOCUS ON RELATIONSHIPS AND INTERESTS

I'm excited to go to a team that has a lot of drivers I can learn from and who know how to win.

—Danica Patrick on her 2006 move from Rahal
Letterman Racing to Andretti Green Racing

"Next question?" Drew Rosenhaus responded over and over as reporters pressed to get deeper insight into the controversy surrounding his client Terrell Owens. Rosenhaus was standing on the front lawn of Owens's Morristown, New Jersey, home, surrounded by cameras and reporters. Owens had just apologized for the series of comments he had made that were not supportive of his team, the Philadelphia Eagles, and its star quarterback, Donovan McNabb.

The negative sound bites started after the team's 2005 loss in Super Bowl XXXIX to the New England Patriots. The last straw came when Owens was asked in an interview whether he believed the Eagles would be undefeated if Brett Favre, the Green Bay Packers quarterback, took over for the Eagles. "That's a good assessment," Owens responded,

"I would agree with that, just with what [Favre] brings to the table."

This was not what anyone expected to hear from one teammate reflecting on another. Was he saying that his teammate McNabb was not up to the task? Almost everybody, led by the powerful Philadelphia talk radio forces, interpreted it that way.

Owens and his agent held what evolved into a huge press conference in front of Owens's home. There Owens apologized to McNabb and his team following Owens's suspension for "conduct detrimental to" the Eagles a few days earlier. Whatever had been undone by the apology was in some sense being revived by Rosenhaus with his now classic "next question" repetition. Rosenhaus was being the zealous advocate and trying to take the media heat on behalf of his client.

Rosenhaus appeared to win no personal public relations points for himself or his client. The commentators were certain that harm had been done to Owens's career that would be difficult, if not impossible, to undo. Those critics may have been correct in terms of endorsements in the short term and certainly about any hopes of a new Eagles contract. But as for Owens's football future, talent trumped any concern for disruption of team chemistry or for representation by Rosenhaus.

Following Owens's suspension, Rosenhaus sought to field offers for a new team for his client. Owens wanted a new deal from the Eagles following his stellar performance in the Super Bowl. He had come back from a broken fibula and ligament damage in his right ankle ahead of schedule and played at a level well above anyone's expectations in that game. As a result, he wanted to renegotiate the deal that was paying him $3.5 million in 2005 as part of a seven-year $49 million contract. Owens argued that the contract was "back-loaded" and that the salary in the first two years did not even place him in the top 10 in salaries for NFL wide receivers.

Ultimately, Rosenhaus negotiated a $25 million three-year contract for his client with the Dallas Cowboys. The deal paid Owens a salary of $5 million as well as a $5 million bonus in the first year. Then in 2008 he entered into a new four-year deal paying him $34 million, including a $12.9 million bonus. Owens has generally continued to play at the highest level. Rosenhaus, by virtue of his style of advocacy and contract negotiation success, also won over a number of future clients. The Eagles is a franchise that has a rigid policy against renegotiating deals that still have time to run, which Owens did. This was a highly risky move by Rosenhaus, which ultimately paid off for him and his client.

Over the years I've learned that players generally love Drew Rosenhaus, and the players are the ones who employ him. Rosenhaus is doing what he considers best in order to have the strongest relationships possible with the people who pay his bills: his football player clients. His attention to detail on behalf of his clients is really at the heart of player loyalty. With a client base hovering at around 100, he is always ready to take calls from players, thanks to his collection of cell phones, which he keeps attached to him at all times. Unlike agent Leigh Steinberg, who spends a huge portion of his career ensuring that his image is as shiny as it can be, Rosenhaus focuses on his relationships with the NFL players and not on anything or anyone else. It is in the interest of his player clients to get the best deals possible. On average they will play in the league for just over three years, and for that reason, it is important for them to get as much money as they can in that time period. Rosenhaus's interests? The same, but also to attract new clients. Relationships and interests are closely intertwined when it comes to factors beyond money in closing deals.

⇥ VALUING RELATIONSHIPS ⇤

Another "nice" agent is Ron Shapiro. (He, in fact, wrote a book called *The Power of Nice*.) Shapiro's likability is genuine and manifests itself in his relationships with his clients. Shapiro's view is that every deal and every party involved in a deal represents a potential beneficial relationship. He famously negotiated contracts for clients Cal Ripken Jr. in Baltimore and Kirby Puckett in Minnesota that had more to do with positive long-term relationships and earning power than short-term dollars and possible alienation of fans. In an era when it is rare for any athlete to spend the bulk of his or her career in one city, these two did, and the common denominator was Shapiro. Uniquely, both ballplayers played in the same city throughout their baseball careers rather than take free-agent dollars in other venues.

Even the person considered the forerunner of all sports agents, Bob Woolf, says that it is important to leave some money on the table. "I haven't done a single contract that I couldn't have gotten more money on. I always leave money on the table." To him, relationships are that important.

If you want a relationship to last, it is important that your negotiating counterparts see that they are receiving some benefit and that you are not pounding them into the ground. The best negotiators incorporate a focus on relationships into their initial preparation as well as during the negotiation itself. But as Rosenhaus illustrates, you need to determine which relationships you want to impact.

⊰ Guanxi ⊱

The relationship issue can be more broadly cultural as well. One of the most marketable athletes of the twenty-first century has to be Yao Ming, the star center of the Houston Rockets and one of the top vote getters for the NBA All-Star Game since his entry into the league in 2002. The story of both how he came to play in the United States and was fortunate enough to become a part of his team involves a web of people who were successful because they understood the value of relationships. "Team Yao" consists of agent Bill Duffy, University of Chicago deputy dean John Huizinga, and University of Chicago Business School graduate student Erik Zhang.

Zhang was dating a woman, now his wife, who said she had a cousin who was a basketball player. His name was Yao Ming. Through a series of circumstances, Zhang elicited the aid of John Huizinga, who was a professor at Chicago. It was Huizinga who ultimately negotiated Yao's NBA player contract. Bill Duffy is the longtime experienced agent who markets Yao Ming. And since, for political reasons, the Chinese Basketball Association required that Yao have an agent in China, there is Lu Hao.

Chinese leadership was reluctant to allow their basketball players to play in the NBA. The most recent experience saw a player come to the United States and not return to China. With an interest in retaining relationships with Yao, the Chinese side was moving cautiously in allowing him to sign any deal, particularly when it came to him playing on the national team in the Olympics. The first concern of the Chinese was who would be allowed to represent Yao and how that person could proceed.

Each party understood the balancing act involved in the negotiation. If either party pressed for something more or different, the entire deal might fall apart. These relationships and connections are captured in the Chinese word *guanxi*. The concept goes beyond old-boy networks, relationships, or connections. *Guanxi* is a network that is developed personally and that, when needed, can be used because of the effort that has been exerted to establish it.

Yao was recognized as an NBA prospect while playing youth basketball in China. The key in recruiting any athlete is having a presence and developing a relationship with the right person. In recruiting players, agents and coaches spend time ensuring they are expending their effort on the right person—whoever is able to influence the athlete to sign on as a client. Sometimes it's an uncle, a mother, or an Amateur Athletic Union (AAU) coach. With Yao, the Chinese government also had influence. The process moved slowly, but all of the parties to the negotiation made the moves necessary to have Yao drafted by a team in a U.S. city with a large Chinese American population: Houston, Texas. This was a key prerequisite to closing the deal. The elements are simply the basics: Who are the decision makers? What is the best way to negotiate with them? A lawyer in the deal summed up what most people came to understand. "For Americans doing a business deal, it's 'Let's do the deal and go.' In China, you don't start doing a deal until you've established a relationship."

These lessons of *guanxi* were not lost on the team that had the opportunity to pursue Yi Jianlian, the man *Time* magazine called "the next Yao Ming." Herb Kohl, the owner of the Milwaukee Bucks (and a U.S. senator), selected Yi sixth in the 2007 NBA draft. The senator, a man well trained in relationships, went right to work on that angle. He had good *guanxi* too. He knew how to deal with Yi's agent. He understood that he had to connect with the decision makers and, as was the case with Yao, that these were people who went beyond the player and his agent.

Reminiscent of the stories of Elway and Manning (see Chapter 4), Yi was not enamored with Milwaukee. It had not been his first choice, as he preferred, like Yao, to play in a city with a large Chinese American community, such as Chicago, Los Angeles, or San Francisco. It also did not help that the Bucks are a small-market team playing in one of the colder NBA climates. Knowing that he was already starting from behind, Kohl moved into action quickly. It is not always the case that an owner, especially one who is a U.S. senator, gets on a plane to personally meet with a potential player. Kohl flew to China and met with Chen Haitao, the owner of the team Yi played for there, as well as with Yi's family and members of the Chinese sports ministry. Money alone was certainly not enough, and Yi had a good bit of leverage in having the option of remaining in China, although without the same financial benefits being offered.

⇥ INTERESTS ⇤

Those most successful in courting relationships take the time and make the effort to understand the interests of their clients. This was certainly done in the cases of Yao and Yi. This depth of understanding was equally important to representing these athletes as it was in signing them to play for their American teams.

That famous little negotiating book *Getting to Yes* uses that focus on understanding the interests of the other side, as opposed to their position, as being the backbone of all negotiating principles. In most deals, this means that you need to comprehend what there is in a relationship with a counterpart, that relationship is important beyond the dollars and cents of the deal.

With Yi, the Chinese sports ministry wanted to be sure that he actually saw some playing time during his first year in Milwaukee. Why was that important? The Olympics were being hosted in Beijing in 2008, and the ministry wanted one of its best players to be ready for that global competition. Yi couldn't be playing a second-rate game because he had been relegated to the bench in his early days with the Bucks. Again, Kohl recognized this need and gave Team Yi personal assurances that it would be met. Developing the relationship and addressing the counterpart's interests aided in closing the deal and bringing Yi to Milwaukee.

⇥ CULTURAL RELATIONSHIP FOCUS ⇤

Both the Yao and Yi negotiations hinged on having an understanding of Chinese culture. In another negotiation, sports agent Arn Tellem found that relationship issues were critical in landing baseball player Hideki Matsui as a client. Tellem's negotiating skills were also important to winning over Matsui.

"I got a call from a firm in Japan first asking me if I knew who Matsui was," Tellem reminisced with a smile. "Of course I did. They then gave me a specific list of questions he wanted answered, and they asked me to write a letter to him."

This was a highly unusual request in baseball, but not in terms of business in Japan. This additional step added time to the traditional agent recruitment of a baseball player, but that was part of what it took to close the deal. Like Senator Kohl in the case of Yi, Tellem got on a plane to meet Matsui and his representatives personally. As a result, Matsui signed with Tellem.

⇥ RELATIONSHIP POWER ⇤

A positive relationship got another deal done when the owners of the Philadelphia basketball and hockey teams, the 76ers and the Flyers, came together under one roof. The year was 1996, and most believed that the then owner of the 76ers basketball team, Harold Katz, had no interest in selling his team. Katz also specifically had no interest in selling the team to the owners of the local hockey team. Yet the owners of the hockey team had a big vision: to ensure content for its infant cable arm, Comcast.

Independent of this interest, Pat Croce had been seeking the rights to buy the 76ers from Katz for quite awhile. Croce was a friend of Katz and also the trainer and owner of the company that did physical therapy for the 76ers and Flyers. Finally, Katz gave Croce a price for the 76ers, a reported $125 million. Croce then was able to bring together the parties, keep a piece for himself, and close a deal that otherwise seemed impossible. Cash alone would not have allowed that deal to close. The deal would not have happened without the Croce-Katz relationship.

⇥ REGAINING RELATIONSHIP FOCUS ⇤

The negotiation between Alex Rodriguez and the New York Yankees in 2007 illustrates both the worst and best understanding of the power of relationships. No one could have anticipated the negotiation that not only would occupy the sports pages but also would end up prominently in the *Wall Street Journal*. Rodriguez had an "out clause" in his Yankees contract. This allowed him to give up the $72 million he was to make over the final three years of his then 10-year $252 million deal. The upside was that this would allow him to negotiate with all 30 Major League Baseball clubs. Even the most amateurish of negotiators understands the type of leverage 29 other suitors can provide.

Inexplicably, at least for any positive strategic reason, the out was exercised during game four of the 2007 World Series. The problem was more the timing than the fact that Rodriguez and his agent, Scott Boras, did it. The teams, commissioner, fans, and players association were all outraged. Also, reports had it that Rodriguez and his wife, Cynthia, wanted to stay in New York, the world's brightest sports stage. Why did they do it?

It was stunning that a player, who many thought would complete his career on the biggest stage in the world, had now pulled the plug. The reasoning made sense—leverage by increasing the potential bidders for his services—but what a negative impact not only on the relationship with the team but also on those associated with the sport of baseball. That included those 29 other teams.

The bidding for his services was reported to be tepid. The expressed price tag of $300 million was so high that the potential bidders decided to stay out of the fray. That is where it began to get interesting. Rodriguez was having second thoughts, and he began to talk with third parties. Athletes in that orbit sometimes have big-name friends, and he had one of the biggest: financier Warren Buffett.

Buffett's advice was purely, solidly, relationship driven: "Talk to the Yankees directly, without your agent." Rodriguez respected Buffett and leaned toward taking that advice. Although Rodriguez was still reluctant to make the call to the Yankees himself, he knew others whom he felt could call the team on his behalf. One rule impeding Rodriguez's progress absent his agent was that third-party intermediaries could not negotiate the deal unless they were certified by the players' union, the Major League Baseball Players Association (MLBPA).

Even with this impediment, Rodriguez contacted Goldman Sachs's private wealth manager, John Mallory. That too was a preexisting relationship. Mallory happened to handle money for the Steinbrenner family, which owns the Yankees. Mallory still did not have the direct link, so he brought in one more person, Gerry Cardinale, a partner at Goldman, who specializes in the media and telecommunications sectors.

The message finally did get through to the Yankees that Rodriguez wanted to talk, first to team president Randy Levine and then to George Steinbrenner. As the *Wall Street Journal* reports said, they would talk with Rodriguez but only if Boras was not involved. There was a lot of frustration, maneuvering, and wasted time because relationships had gone south, but eventually Rodriguez was back with the Yankees. He got there because he took additional steps when the relationship that was in place no longer functioned. Rodriguez eventually did re-sign with the Yankees for $275 million over 10 years.

⇥ INTERESTS BEYOND THE MONEY ⇤

The experiences of many athletes help us to understand that it's not always about the money. For some, it's about championships; for others, it's about playing on stages different and bigger than the ones they are accustomed to. For example, in 2007, Sidney Crosby signed a five-year $43.5 million contract with the Pittsburgh Penguins hockey team. He could have demanded 20 percent of the then salary cap ceiling of $50.3 million or $10.06 million per year for four years. He did not because he wanted to enable the Penguins to sign more young talent in order to become more competitive. Sure, money was important, but a big part of his interest was winning.

Another person this brings to mind is Danica Patrick and her move from one racing team to another. Her deal with the Rahal Letterman Racing team was ending in 2006. Rumors were swirling not only about her leaving for another Indy Racing League (IRL) team but also about the possibility of her jumping to the National Association for Stock Car Auto Racing (NASCAR). In many ways Patrick had become one of the hottest properties in racing, because of both her good looks and up-and-coming driving skills. She set forth her priority, which went beyond money. "I want to win in IndyCar. I want to win the Indy 500. I want to do well." She continued, "If there's a team in the series that will give me that opportunity, this is where I'll be." With this in mind, she moved to the Andretti Green Racing team. "I'm joining the winningest team in the series," she declared. Patrick proved her desire to win by being the first female to win an IRL race: the Japan 300 in 2008.

Another example that was certainly about money but also about new possibilities was David Beckham's move from Real Madrid to the Los Angeles Galaxy of Major League Soccer (MLS). He entered a much-publicized five-year deal worth $250 million. Beckham earns up to $10 million a year in direct salary, but with endorsements and profit sharing he really makes in the neighborhood of $50 million. "I want to play at the highest level for a few more years yet. I've got that planned out; going to America is one of the ideas that I've thought of in the future." This was the way Beckham described his future.

Indy Racing League driver Danica Patrick

Why would David Beckham leave Europe to play in the United States where soccer isn't nearly as watched or respected? The answer is simple, as the former U.S. soccer star and current manager of the Los Angeles Galaxy, Alexi Lalas, said: "He's an entertainment personality who draws paparazzi like a movie star, regularly finding his way onto tabloid and magazine covers. With snazzy clothes, rotating hair colors and styles, and a pop star wife, he is the epitome of the modern mix of celebrity and athlete. He's even had a movie named after him: *Bend It Like Beckham*, released three years ago." David Beckham had his self-interest in mind. So when he chose to play for the Los Angeles Galaxy, he chose that team based on the publicity he would receive as well as on the money he would be paid. That's what his interest was.

In 2003, before the Yankees deal in 2007, Alex Rodriguez and his agent, Scott Boras, had a negotiation that focused on interests as well. "I said, 'There may be an opportunity. We have to talk about your goals, about winning,'" Boras recalled telling his client. At the time, Rodriguez played for the Texas Rangers.

If he stayed with Texas, he would earn the remaining $67 million on his 10-year contract but probably would not win any championships. With the Yankees, Rodriguez had the opportunity to play on a team that would give him a greater chance of winning the World Series. This trade resulted in an increased value to Rodriguez, which worked to his self-interest.

This deal was complicated further because there was also a position change involved, from shortstop to third base, so as not to displace Derek Jeter, the All-Star shortstop

Global soccer superstar David Beckham

for the Yankees. Although Rodgriguez was a Gold Glove–winning shortstop and most people didn't think that he would agree to the switch, Rodriguez did so for a chance to play in a World Series. This was the way to align interests: if Rodriguez would change positions, the Yankees could provide him with the World Series opportunity.

⇥ Aligning Interests ⇤

One issue that is occurring with greater frequency is the decision athletes have to make between playing for a club team or for their country. We have seen a form of this recently in the United States, with professionals having an opportunity to play on Olympic baseball and basketball teams, but it is an even bigger issue in other countries. Cricket and rugby are two global sports that have had this "club-versus-country" dilemma.

In rugby since 1995, the struggle has been between the rugby clubs in the English Premiership and the Rugby Football Union, which governs the British national team. The first major conflict with these players occurred when the clubs refused to release their players to tour New Zealand and Australia with the national team. The challenge is to align the interests of all the parties.

The key to solving this conflict has been both to work on the relationships among the parties and also to understand the interests of everybody, particularly the athletes. Whether it is accommodating schedules, reducing the number of events the athletes must participate in, or adjusting compensation, all of these elements must be addressed. The more highly compensated the athlete, the less important is the idea of an even higher salary. Often a patriotic appeal can make the difference. This aligning of interests is the vital key to relationship building. If you have taken the time to understand the interests of your counterparts in a negotiation, you can achieve greater success if you align your interests with theirs.

A big part of Don King's success in bringing together Ali and Foreman, discussed in Chapter 4, was about understanding the interests and egos of both men. Each boxer was told that he was earning $500,000 more than the other: Foreman because he was the legitimate champion and Ali because he was "the people's champ." This satisfied the ego of both. But the interest for Foreman was to be the true champion, to silence Ali; for Ali, it was the chance to regain the title.

King also played what has come to be referred to as "the race card." Nearing the end of his 90-minute sales pitch to Foreman, after discussing money and still not convincing Foreman to come on board, King pointed to Foreman's skin and said: "You're two super athletes. Both black. You've got to forgo the pettiness. This event is bigger than both of you as individuals. It's monumental, not just in revenue but in symbolic impact that will reverberate throughout the world—from a black perspective. This is *my* promotion! And I'm *black*! Here is an opportunity to give inspiration to the downtrodden, to show that black men, together, can succeed with proficiency and effectiveness."

With that, Foreman signed three blank sheets of paper, giving King the authority to put the contract together.

In creating your game plan, leave adequate time for thinking about relationships. The value of those relationships will be individual as well as cultural. If you are negotiating in another country, or with someone from a different country, be aware of the special issues that might be presented by virtue of this diversity. Closely coupled with relationships is the importance of understanding the interests of the other side and those associated with them. Often those interests, the real reasons why someone wants to get a deal done, are nonmonetary. The two are intertwined, as you cannot always get to a party's interests unless you extend the effort to develop a relationship.

⇥ RELATIONSHIPS IMPACTING ⇤ FUTURE NEGOTIATIONS

I had the occasion to speak with an NBA team executive during a crucial negotiation for a key player. The agent the team was battling was making a very aggressive salary demand. He was also threatening that the player he represented would go elsewhere if the team did not meet the demand.

The NBA team executive reminded me that his front office was young and that he was concerned about two things: how the NBA was coming across to this agent and how this deal would impact future transactions. His questions showed a lot of insight.

I began to advise him on the NBA's future reputation in the marketplace. "The salary is the least important part of this deal." I paused. This was a bit of an overstatement. The money part of a deal is, of course, always important, and it is not likely that sports executives would ever lose sight of it. "This is really going to put a stake in the ground on how agents will deal with you and your organization going forward." He was taking this in, and mentioned that he and his fellow NBA executives were meeting on this issue in just a few moments. "What you really need to do is agree as a team to your walk-away point, be sure the agent knows what your walk-away point is, and then do not cave."

This would be a huge message about the marketplace for that team. I also thought the team needed the incentive to call the agent's bluff, while at the same time clearly establishing the bottom line internally. This was a step to getting the team in the habit of doing negotiation planning. Sometimes we are sending messages to affect relationships that we do not yet have in place. They did ultimately sign that player at their walk-away point.

Fully contemplate the importance of current and future negotiations. Make sure, too, that you understand your counterpart's true interest in closing the deal. To be a successful negotiator, you must embrace the negotiating process and be fully engaged in seeking the best deal your circumstances allow.

⇥ Takeaways ⇤

1. Focus on the value of relationships in every negotiation.
2. Have good *guanxi*, or connections.
3. Be aware that developing relationships can lead to uncovering interests, and vice versa.
4. Align those interests with those of your counterpart whenever possible.
5. Understand that you never know whom you may be dealing with next.
6. Understand the real interests of your counterpart and how fulfilling those may positively affect your relationship and potentially close the deal.

CHAPTER 6

EMBRACE THE
BARGAINING PROCESS

I've been playing baseball for a long time . . . every time I've
heard the umpire get ready to start a game, he always says,
"Play ball!" I've never once heard him say, "Work ball."

—Willie Stargell, baseball Hall of Famer

"On the big deals, I like to meet in person initially," Octagon's Phil de Picciotto says regarding going into the bargaining process. Octagon is one of the dominant firms in the sports marketing and management business, with clients including Olympian Michael Phelps and football's John Elway. "It's very important in terms of information gathering. In the first encounter I make an effort not to discuss the deal itself but to talk around the deal and the elements." This is all part of relationship building, gearing up to the negotiation. But serious information can be acquired at this preliminary stage as well.

"This approach can be a bit disarming," admits de Picciotto. In the next communication, he likes to move the negotiation forward. "How would you like to start this negotiation?" In addition to the agenda, part of what de Picciotto specifically wants to get to is the negotiation format: "Are you going to start high and me low, or can we get right to the reasonable numbers or elements?" Every negotiation, however, is different.

"Assuming both sides are reasonable," says de Picciotto, "it can be an intellectual and highly enjoyable process." In the best of circumstances both sides realize there is not a "sale" but a form of coming together based on mutual interests. The negotiation merely establishes the terms of that union, but it can be difficult to see that at times.

Once the process is underway, your preparation must kick in. "You're the experts; you know the market. We just know baseball. You tell us." So said sports agent Ron Shapiro to a book publisher. In this deal, however, he was representing Cal Ripken Jr. and the rights to a book on his life story. Shapiro is adamant about not wanting to make the opening offer, and he relates the following story to ensure that we understand his reasoning.

Cal Ripken Jr. was asked continually about his interest in writing an autobiography. Here was the future Major League Baseball Hall of Famer who was on the verge of breaking and who eventually did break one of the most important records in sports: Lou Gehrig's mark of 2,130 consecutive games. Shapiro's research had found that the typical life story of a pro athlete was purchased by publishers for $500,000. Shapiro correctly assessed that, at this moment, Ripken was extraordinary and should be paid accordingly. In preparing, Shapiro placed the value of Ripken's story at $700,000.

This "you-tell-us" approach turned out to be an ideal move. The first offer of the publisher Shapiro approached was for $750,000. Taking it one step further, Shapiro was prepared for the surprise and did not act in a manner revealing his initial position; he simply responded, "I'll get back to you."

After countering at $1,250,000, the Cal Ripken Jr. autobiography sold for $1,000,000. Shapiro had a vision of the entire process, trusted his plan, and revised it when he gained new information while negotiating.

This was all part of being flexible in the negotiation process. Go in knowing that new information will be forthcoming in the course of the negotiation and be ready to readjust even the best-mapped-out goals. The practice is wide ranging, but the actual act requires patience. There has to be a grasp of the way the discussion will ebb and flow and an understanding of the rhythm. Much of the success you will have depends upon whether you are fully engaged in the negotiation process and whether you absorb all of the additional information that makes itself available.

EXPERT TIP

Knowing where you want to end up is easy to prepare,
the hard part is how to get there.
That is the more important, difficult part.

— Phil de Picciotto, president,
Octagon, Athletes & Personalities

⇥ NEGOTIATIONS ARE NERVE-RACKING ⇤

After having read the chapter title "Embrace the Bargaining Process," you might have said to yourself, "Negotiations are nerve-racking; what do you mean "embrace"? By "embrace" I mean fully understand and immerse yourself in the process—working to get to the point that you look forward to a negotiation as much as you looked forward to playing your favorite sports as a youth. Over and over when I played team sports, I heard coaches focus on making game day fun, on getting the players to realize that this is what it has all been about. The extensive practice. The weight training. The discipline. It's like all those years in the driveway or park, playing in the frame of mind of joyful youth. The ideal would be to reach that same level of enjoyment with bargaining. Can you visualize that? No? Well, that is what you are striving for. For most people, the endeavor is not easy.

I'm not sure Alex Rodriguez embraced or enjoyed bargaining for himself with the Yankees (see Chapter 5), but he had no choice. And when we are thrust into negotiating, absent a specific innate competitive style that will allow us to enjoy bargaining, most of us probably don't want to do it. Likewise, we're usually not going to enjoy something unless we are successful at it.

Athletes will often practice for hours the one move, shot, stroke, or whatever they have hated to do the most. At some point, that move may actually become their favorite, or what they do best. One way to get there—to the point of embracing—is practice. I often tell my students to practice negotiating, particularly in those settings in which there is not a lot on the line—for example, taxi fares. Negotiate a flat rate with the driver before you start moving. If the driver refuses to negotiate, you pay the meter; if he or she negotiates, you get practice and maybe save a couple of bucks. While paying for your purchases at the department store, ask the clerk if there is a discount available. You may be told that a sale starts tomorrow, but the salesperson will honor it for you today. Or you may be offered the opportunity to speak to the store manager. As with just about any other activity, the more you do it, the more comfortable you become at it.

The previous chapters have given you the key pieces to becoming a successful bargainer. Pat Summitt amplifies what Tony Dungy said about the little things. Her message is about not being too focused on the end result, but as Dungy points out, it is the little things along the way that lead to winning. Summitt correctly suggests, "Above all, the experience of going undefeated . . . reaffirmed the importance of doing the little things. . . . When you want to win a championship, you don't focus on winning. You focus on the small tasks you have to do in order to win."

Once they begin their professional careers, it is rare that people have the opportunity to practice their negotiating skills with individuals outside of their jobs. When I teach executives or students I remind them, "This is a tax-free opportunity for you to get better at this." The more they do it, the less trepidation they have about doing it the next time.

⇥ PREPARATION WILL BRING CONFIDENCE ⇤

The negotiation process will get easier and more enjoyable. What you don't want to do is lose sight of the basics in the process. Let's start with thinking again about the importance of preparation versus winging it. Do you ever reach a point where preparation is not necessary? No. To be the best you can be, preparation is essential. It may be that you don't have time to prepare before every negotiation. That happens. But when you can prepare, you should.

There is a great lesson to be learned from the San Francisco 49ers Hall of Fame quarterback Joe Montana. Head coach Bill Walsh installed the offense of the 49ers the same way every season, beginning with the same play. Imagine players sitting around and hearing every detail of how a play is to be executed, from beginning to end, and learning how the play is designed to set up success for the next play. And even though he has heard Walsh explain the offense so many times before and it would be easy to tune him out, Montana listens and takes notes just as though he were a rookie. Preparation. This is a necessary part of embracing not only the actual negotiation but also the entire process.

Montana illustrates one additional point. For most of us, if a task has become old hat or repetitious, we rarely take the time to prepare, as evidenced by the statements "I've sold this policy a million times," "I know this program inside and out," and "I've dealt with this customer a dozen times." Montana had won the Super Bowl, but he prepared as though he had never played in it before, and he went on to win again. Would greater preparation improve your success ratio? Evidence shows that it is worth a try.

⇥ MAKING THE OPENING OFFER ⇤

In preparing, one of the big things to decide is whether or not you will make the opening offer. Should you do it? As your negotiating confidence increases, you will get to the point where you more fully appreciate the positives of opening first. We discussed this topic a bit in Chapter 3, where Ueberroth's setting the floor of his negotiation was essentially a way of opening. For those of you who never think about making the opening offer, tell yourself that in the preparation stage of your negotiation, you will give it thorough consideration.

Certainly, being able to open is predicated on your style as well as on the amount of information you have. For some, it will be virtually impossible to take the initiative. Making the opening offer can be difficult, but doing so can be a powerful tool. On the flip side, as Shapiro showed, there are times when waiting is good. Both Ueberroth and Shapiro made great moves. You must fully evaluate which tactic will bring you success. The basic logic is that opening first makes the most sense when you have the same amount of, or perhaps even more, information than your opponent does. The only reason you may want your opponent to "go first" when you have more information? To see if misinformation or a wrongly held belief will get you an offer that is wildly in your favor.

Your preparation really drives your enjoyment and success. Taking your time and setting an appropriate goal can protect you against an inappropriate opening by your counterpart. One of the key advantages to opening first is *anchoring*, a well-established negotiating technique. The party who puts the first proposal on the table can anchor, or focus, the conversation around his or her initial position. The Ueberroth approach to setting a floor in a negotiation represents a form of anchoring.

Much has been written about the power of anchoring. Many studies show that a fair opening tends to dictate where a deal will end up. The best way to counter an offer that should not have the power to anchor? To immediately discredit the offer. Only those who are prepared are able to do so.

Once you make an offer, you should wait until you get a response from the other side. You do not want to end up in a circumstance where you are negotiating against yourself.

❧ THE RECIPROCAL OFFER ❦
OR COUNTEROFFER

What do you do next? Much of the answer depends on how you prefer to negotiate and how you have assessed your counterpart. If the other side opens at a number that is not within the *positive bargaining zone*, as defined by you, acknowledge that you are aware of that. It does little good to come back with an equally absurd counteroffer. What I like to do is convince the other side that the only fair course of action is for them to make a valid offer within the zone. You may not always be able to make that happen, but it is certainly worth the effort. What should you do if an outrageous initial offer is placed before you? Phil de Picciotto gives some possible responses:

"What am I missing here?"

"Do you really want to make a deal?"

Generally de Picciotto is a collaborative problem solver. Here, he becomes a bit of a chameleon to try and move the negotiation forward without giving any ground. This is a much more competitive tone.

The Shapiro example at the beginning of the chapter gives you much to think about in positioning your counter-offer. If you did not open, what response do you give to the opening you receive? Your reaction depends upon your preparation. But your preparation is now enhanced by the additional information you received during the course of the negotiation.

W. David Cornwell, a longtime sports lawyer, gives a good example of how to deal with a competitive party's counteroffer: "When I worked at the Upper Deck Company, I was negotiating a royalty deal against the agent for a big-name player. When it came to the percentage, he said that he wanted 30 percent of the revenues. It was clear they were not going to budge from that figure." This was multiple percentages higher than the typical numbers for a deal of this type.

This agent had a reputation for being competitive and getting what he wanted. Cornwell had a strategy in mind: "We went back and worked on a definition of revenues that would give him the 30 percent. We focused on the details of the definition; he focused on the percentage. We satisfied his ego and at the same time got a good deal for the company by loading every expense we could into the revenue definition that the 30 percent was drawn from." This is both great creativity and a great counteroffer.

⇥ Don't Force a Deal ⇤

One of my first clients was a young tennis player, who had done fairly well at the sport during her four years in college. However, as many people know, the fact that someone plays collegiate tennis for four years is a modern-day indicator that that person might not go far in the women's game. My client thought that she might be in a position to get an offer from a tennis racket company, and she asked me to approach the firm on her behalf. I was still a young, relatively inexperienced lawyer at the time, and I agreed to do it.

The company's representative said, "Sure, we'd be interested in working with her." I was a bit surprised at how enthusiastic the rep was, and I should have probed more deeply to really understand his interest. I was moving too quickly, anxious to close a favorable deal.

"Great, how can I be helpful in putting together a deal for her?" I asked, hoping to get a bit more insight on what the company was willing to provide my client. Here was a setting in which I was fishing for the goal, target, and walk-away point. I knew we should be going somewhere north of being compensated with equipment only, but I was not at all sure what the possibilities were.

The rep then seemed a bit rushed and said, "Just send me over your contract and we'll see where we can go from there." This sounded simple, but he knew and I knew there was no "form" contract out there for this particular level of player. I gave it some thought, talked with the client and others at length, and decided to send the rep a contract that started with the basic equipment but included bonuses for top-level rankings and victories in Grand Slam tournaments.

I mailed the contract, and the only response I got was silence. I did not want to appear anxious, so I waited. And waited. I told my client I was a little concerned, and then I called.

The representative answered the phone, and I identified myself. "Who?" he said. Mr. Friendly was now in a very sarcastic mood. "Look, I don't know who you think you are representing, but we're not interested in any Taj Mahal contract for her." I began to explain that I was just looking for a starting point for our conversation. All he wanted to do was make it clear that I had not provided the anchor. At the end of our discussion he offered equipment only, and we closed.

⇥ LISTEN ⇤

What I failed to do was listen—or at least pause long enough for the other side to give me more insight. I failed to go deeper. I needed to extract more information from my opposite. The outcome might have been better had I simply prepared a list of probing questions. I assumed too much and moved based on my desire (getting a great deal) rather than on reality (settling for equipment only). Shapiro also delivers the message that a big component of successful negotiating is listening. And listening not only for opening numbers but also for other things said throughout the conversation.

The hard work is in eliciting information from the other side. The successful way to do this may have been best stated by the businessperson Malcolm Forbes. It is about listening: "To seduce almost anyone, ask for and listen to his [or her] opinion." Cornwell takes it a step further: "You should remain silent to the point of discomfort. You never know what information the other side will reveal if they feel they need to keep talking."

The ultimate fear, the reason we may talk too much and not listen enough, is the fear of not making a deal. However, if we have clearly established our walk-away point and no data have come in to change it, walking away is not a bad thing.

EXPERT TIP

At some point in every negotiation you have to say where you are going, and then there's no more. Otherwise there won't be any resolution.

—David Stern, NBA commissioner

⇥ Be Creative ⇤

There are times when a deal is not coming together. Every deal of that type is not necessarily a stalemate or one you should walk away from. If parties truly want to make a deal, all that may be called for is a high level of creativity.

The sports business is full of great deals—for example, basketball players Wilt Chamberlain and later Kareem Abdul-Jabbar being traded to the Los Angeles Lakers, and back even further, Babe Ruth being traded from the Boston Red Sox to the New York Yankees for only $125,000. The contract bringing Alex Rodriguez to the Yankees probably deserves to be listed up there as well. No one knew that Rodriguez would move from shortstop to third base. You can even lump the dramatic increase in the size of sports sponsorship deals into this category. But there is one deal that spans the ages for both its overall value and the way the deal makers had foresight beyond all others in the terms they crafted. It was also highly creative and a bit speculative, but it did turn out well for both sides.

Ozzie and Dan Silna, the owners of the Spirits of St. Louis, a basketball team in the defunct American Basketball Association (ABA), continue to get paid, over 30 years later, in what might be the greatest long-term sports deal ever.

One big sports deal everyone wants, and which few have had the opportunity to achieve, is the one in which an upstart league merges with the surviving entity. Much of what Donald Trump was trying to do with the old United States Football League (USFL) was to position that franchise for the merger opportunity. (For more details, see Chapter 7.) There had been successful deals in the past with the American Football League (AFL)–National Football League (NFL) merger in 1970 and the American Basketball Association(ABA)–National Basketball Association (NBA) merger in 1976.

No one understood how great the ABA deal was for the Spirits of St. Louis. When the NBA and ABA were negotiating a merger, only four of the remaining six ABA teams would be merged into the league. The other two teams, including the Spirits of St. Louis, had to be compensated according to the ABA bylaws. In the deal, the other team accepted a $3.3 million onetime payment. The Silnas received $3 million and one-seventh of the national television revenues in perpetuity from each of the four teams that did merge. Little did the Silnas, or anyone else, know that it would be extraordinary. The Silnas have already earned nearly $200 million.

Also ranking up there in terms of creativity is a deal for the acquisition of a professional soccer franchise. A conglomeration of 28,000 sports fans from 70 countries joined via their Web site, www.myfootballclub.co.uk, to explore the purchase of a soccer team. They each paid £35, or about $68, for an annual membership to the Web site, which gave them an interest in a team via their MyFootballClub Trust. This money not only provided the funding for the purchase but also established an instant fan base of at least 28,000 people. The search ended in the purchase of a fifth-tier English soccer team, Ebbsfleet United. The common interest of the 28,000 members was to be an owner. Without their coming together, most of them never would have been able to do that.

The shareholders of Ebbsfleet United had to agree to this takeover at the price of £635,000, or about $1,231,900. They did so because of the appeal to their interests. Revenue was one part; the expanded fan base, another. MyFootballClub Trust ended up with a 75 percent interest in the team.

Existing sponsors loved the idea. The team had been losing £30,000 per year before the purchase of the stake by the Web site members. After the acquisition, Ebbsfleet United went from obscurity to limelight by virtue of visits by television crews from Russia, Brazil, Mexico, and Sweden.

As is almost always the case in the best of deals, who knew? My golf buddy has a saying he likes to throw out whenever I make one of those rare great shots on the course: "Every now and then even a hobo pulls a whole chicken out of the garbage can."

⊰ Closing ⊱

I think one of the most overlooked parts of the deal is the closing, perhaps because there is a level of excitement in the air that comes when the end of the negotiation is finally in sight. But we should all be aware that there is room to improve the deal at the end, possibly for *all* parties.

Once price has been agreed upon, the form of payment, the timing of delivery, the place, and other details may be very important to the other side, but of little relevance to you. You have to continue to fish until the very end.

Here's one final step. In negotiation jargon it's called the "postsettlement negotiation." Assume the deal is done. You may have even signed a draft contract. Here's the phrase that you might consider offering: "Is there any way we can tweak this deal so that we can all be better off?" You certainly won't want to do this at the end of every deal, particularly when there is a chance the deal might blow up if you give the slightest inkling that it might be reopened. But where the relationship is cordial, and your counterpart is collaborative, you might reach an even better deal than the one you closed on.

⇥ TRUST YOUR PREPARATION ⇤

Finally, Coach Wooden presses further on the idea of preparing to perform and not focusing on the opponent when he says, "Don't be too concerned with regard to things over which you have no control, because that will eventually have an adverse effect on things over which you have control."

In order to accomplish what this chapter suggests, you must be prepared. Confidence will play a big role in your negotiations, and you may not get that confidence until you do a few deals. Willie Stargell makes the key point at the

Hall of Famer Willie Stargell playing ball

beginning of this chapter. No matter the activity, you are more likely to be successful at it if you enjoy doing it rather than if you consider it to be work.

⇥ Takeaways ⇤

1. Enjoy the negotiation more by being fully prepared.
2. Know that practice is key.
3. Move at a pace that requires the other side to adjust to you.
4. Gather information as you go, and adjust your game plan if you see possible gains.
5. Be innovative. Enjoy creativity.
6. Trust your walk-away point.
7. Trust your preparation.

CHAPTER 7

HANDLE OTHER PEOPLE'S BUSINESS

That's what agents are for.

—Latrell Sprewell, then of the New York Knicks,
when asked why he failed to inform his
team and teammates about missing a week of
practice prior to the 1999–2000 NBA season

I once assisted an incoming tennis coach at a major university in the negotiation of his contract. When the coach called to hire me, we discussed all of the details of what he wanted, comparables, salaries, and other related matters. As I was asking him about his contact person at the university, he became a little tentative. "I think we'd be better off if I did the talking myself," the tennis coach told me.

Apparently, when he had raised the issue of his attorney calling to discuss the deal, the point person on the other side had said, "I don't do agents."

There is often a negative view of attorneys and an even worse one of sports agents. Agents for coaches at the collegiate level are not as commonplace as they are at the professional level, at least not for sports other than football and basketball. It was certainly possible that this university official had never dealt with an agent, so it was not shocking that he was reluctant to deviate from his normal negotiation practice.

I told my client that the main reasons to use an agent were to get his or her expertise and to have a buffer in any future relationship. My gut feeling was that if I were to contact the university official, the negotiation would be easier to conduct than if my client negotiated directly with someone who had more experience in these matters. My client was convinced that there would be more harm in bringing me in than there would be in me keeping in the background. He was the client, and as we talked, I became confident that in the end we could do just as well with him instead of with me. Part of why I thought it would work was that there were so few elements requiring negotiation. Also, my client was quite competent in business dealings, and I felt that he could handle the deal—with my guidance.

Before fully agreeing to the negotiation plan, I warned my client to consider any harm this negotiation might do to the ongoing relationship he would have with the university once hired. Although I reminded him again that this was one of the primary reasons to use an agent, I was also keenly aware that the use of agents can sometimes be detrimental.

In thinking about this hesitancy on the part of the other side to interact with a third party, I relayed an apocryphal

Legendary NFL coach Vince Lombardi

story about Green Bay Packers coach Vince Lombardi and his 1960s view of agents. Lombardi is one of the greatest figures in coaching lore, and, as with John Wooden, there are scores of business management books that look to his style of leadership and motivation to guide business leaders. As the story goes, Lombardi is facing the prospect of having to negotiate with an agent rather than directly with one of his players, center Jim Ringo. Ringo arrives for his annual salary negotiation with Lombardi in the coach's capacity as chief contract negotiator, and when Ringo enters the room with a gentleman wearing a tie, Lombardi asks who the man is. Ringo responds, "My agent." Lombardi excuses himself, steps into the next room, and when he comes back tells Ringo that he is negotiating with the wrong team because he has just been traded to Philadelphia.

Now my client and I certainly did not view the university official as another Lombardi, but we did understand that there was a similarity in that both wanted to maintain the status quo, at least in terms of how this university negotiated in the past. With that backdrop and my client's concerns in mind, we took another approach. We devised a plan for my client to conduct the negotiation via e-mail. I would suggest the text for the e-mails coming from his account, trying to foresee and avoid any mistakes.

The school provided the first offer, so it was pretty easy to move from there. We prepared an e-mail citing the public salaries at other schools and stating where my client's salary should be relative to those, based on his experience and other unique circumstances. We closed the deal with a great outcome, and the university staffer was not unnecessarily put off by having to deal with an agent. My client and I understood our counterpart's style, accommodated it, maintained the relationship, and actually met our goal. All along our thought was that if everything did not go smoothly, I would take over the negotiation directly. That, however, turned out to be unnecessary.

⇥ AGENT PROBLEMS ⇤

Over the years I have written a lot about sports agents and their business, which in large part is a business of relationships. And it is the player-agent relationship from which you can learn a lot about being an "agent" or a "principal" and about getting the best outcome possible in deals. We all have instances where someone negotiates for us or we are negotiating on behalf of someone else. This negotiation skill is also valuable for when we are hiring lawyers or other personal representatives, including real estate agents. I am always reminded about real estate when I think about having someone else look out for my interests.

"It's great that you are prepared to have me write this offer up for you," the real estate agent told my client as he was buying his first home, "but I want you to know that we have another number coming in from another buyer, and I expect that it will be substantially higher than your offer." The agent looked at my client with concern, "I want you to get this house."

I'm not sure at what point it became clear to me that agents generally did not get paid unless their deals closed. But I do remember pulling my client aside and urging him not to increase his offer based on this eleventh-hour fear-mongering. Further, the agent's percentage was not greatly affected by a swing in price of a few thousand dollars up or down. His primary interest was to close the deal.

Closing the deal is a major part of the financial incentive for sports agents. They get paid when the deal is closed, not before. They also get paid more if they renegotiate a deal and there is a new big signing bonus paid to the athlete; the agent gets his or her standard percentage of what might be a multi-million-dollar bonus.

For the sports agent, this financial incentive may cause the relationship aspect of the deal to be all but forgotten. Recall that the relationships that are most important to the athlete are less so to the agent (see Chapter 5). The athlete needs to maintain a strong working relationship with management and the coaches. The agent may have future negotiations with a team, but for the most part there is little harm in having an adversarial edge between them. The agent's primary goal is not to get on the field on game day, but that attitude cannot spill over to the point where it harms the client. That is the place at which relationship interests align, but not before then.

The misalignment of interests is particularly evident when it comes to the athlete's post-playing career when, most likely, the agent's income will no longer depend on the long-term public perception of the client. After the athlete's playing days are over, will he or she be remembered as a greedy money grubber or as the person who was the team player and restructured her or his contract for the benefit of the franchise and the city? This is what was exceptional about the Ron Shapiro deals I mentioned in Chapter 5. In most circumstances, a key concern in using agents is that the interest of the agent and that of the principal are not always aligned. Is this the case with your employees? Your attorneys? Your real estate agent? You? Is the proper incentive in place in these relationships?

Whatever parties may be working with you in a transaction, focus on ways to align your interests. For the real estate agent mentioned earlier, for example, you might pay a bonus related to the agent's finding a deal for a property at a specific price, in addition to his or her percentage. If you are an employer, you might give your employees bonuses for achieving goals above and beyond the call of duty. If your employees know that they may get something extra if they work a bit harder and close a deal at a better data point, not only will the company benefit, but they will too.

⇥ Should You Use an Agent? ⇤

As with my tennis coach client, some preliminary assessment of the prevalence of agents is a valid first move. Whether in real estate, sports, or another business, you need to decide when to use a third party to close a deal for you. What factors should you consider in making your determination? Athletes and entertainers commonly use agents, but the decision to do so is not always based on the particulars of an individual athlete's case; most often the decision is reached based on the notion that "everyone else is doing it, so why shouldn't I?"

There are numerous studies that explore when it is best to use an agent. The leading scholarly article on the topic is called "When Should We Use Agents?" In it the authors say, "When special expertise is required, when tactical flexibility is deemed important and—most importantly—when direct contact is likely to produce confrontation rather than collaboration."

Obviously, in thinking about having an employee represent you, the issues are different and simple: you cannot do it all yourself. In this instance, you are using an employee as an agent for a practical reason related to work allocation. Still, whether dealing with a traditional agent or an employee in your stead, you must make sure your interests are aligned with that person's in order to achieve the outcome that you want in a given negotiation.

⇥ Aligning Interests and Messages ⇤

If you do choose to be represented by a third party for any or all of the reasons mentioned, or if you are simply an employer sending someone out on the company's behalf, the key is to have that person buy into your philosophy, or you must buy into that person's. If your third party does not have interests that are aligned with yours, he or she is not the right person to negotiate for you. Similarly, you might buy into his or her plan to get the outcome that you desire, even if it does not mesh with your negotiating philosophy. My tennis coach client and I were perfectly aligned, but I had another situation several years ago that did not proceed so smoothly. I was the chairman of a committee formed by the then mayor of Philadelphia, John Street, to determine how and where to build new stadiums for the city's professional football and baseball teams.

"Mr. Mayor," I said, "quietly talk to the leaders of the Chinatown community. If there is a joint announcement between you and them . . . that's where we need to be." For some reason, I really believed the mayor was going to do as I suggested because I had thought long and hard about how to steer him toward my position. I was sure my advice was sound. The mayor replied, "Don't worry." And as we sometimes do, I heard what I wanted to hear, which was something like, "I'm going to do what you suggest." The year was 2000.

The mayor did not have the quiet closed-door conversation with the community where we would have given our recommendations about the stadiums. Instead, someone leaked a story to the press, and the community forces were agitating against the idea. The further irony is that while I recognized early on that I was the mayor's agent, I never dreamed that someday he would be perceived as my agent. When the mayor chose not to have closed-door sessions with Chinatown's leaders, the citizens of Philadelphia, especially those of Chinatown, believed that the mayor and I thought alike. When the mayor began to speak publicly on the issue, they believed that he was speaking for me.

Here's what happened: Twenty-two of the cutest little Chinese American kids sat almost directly across from me. They were adorable, and they hated me. They hated me because I was the chairman of the committee that was suggesting that a new ballpark for the Philadelphia Phillies be built in downtown Philadelphia at a site adjacent to Chinatown (not really *in* it, as the newspapers, talk radio personalities, and activists began to forcefully proclaim). Little did I know that the idea of building anything anywhere near Chinatown was a political hot potato in Philadelphia.

I had a calm conversation with the mayor during which I suggested that there needed to be some backroom politics, some discussion with the people of the Chinatown community about what benefits and trade-offs could be won. The mayor chose not to heed my advice.

I gave a brief opening statement at the hearing, trying to shield myself and the other committee members with the label "Citizen Volunteer." That distancing did not help. All the world knew was that this committee made the recommendation to displace these innocent people. Once a public message is delivered, it's difficult to backtrack. I will discuss this more in the next chapter. When you are handling other people's business, make sure the party you are working for is in agreement with you. In this case, the mayor and I disagreed on the approach, but I did not probe enough to really understand the steps that he was going to take. In the end, the ballpark was built not near Chinatown, but in the same sports complex as the previous ballpark in the South Philadelphia section of the city.

⊰ Manage Expectations ⊱

The best sports agents tell me how much time they spend with their athlete clients to get them to understand the financial landscape. They walk through their preparations of comparable player salaries that will be used to close their deals. It is always a good idea to immerse yourself as much as possible in the data related to a given transaction. The phrase "underpromise and overperform" is so important in settings where you are working for others. Taking the time on the front end will reap benefits throughout the negotiating process. As an employee, once you gain new information in the field, report to management the changing circumstances that could ultimately impact the deal that is being sought.

EXPERT TIP

The key is to make certain that your client knows where the deal is likely to end up, and if circumstances change along the way, inform the client. It is imperative that you manage expectations.

—Bill Strickland, president–basketball, Blue Entertainment Sports Television

---

⊰ Partners ⊱

One final thought on the role of agents has to do with business partnerships, but not necessarily in the legal sense. In addition to an agent, you are also likely to allow a business partner to wield negotiating power on your behalf. The business partnership could range anywhere from that found in a law practice to a medical firm to an ice cream business. Many of the same rules that apply to being represented by someone or representing someone in sports apply equally to relationships in the business environment. Within business-es, the partner or business associates are not only constantly negotiating among themselves but also negotiating for each other in transactions with other entities.

You do need to know as thoroughly as possible the person whom you choose to be your partner. You don't want any regrets later on. A focus on relationships and interests can prove invaluable in forming these long-term alliances. These are the people who will be representing your interests, sometimes without there being adequate time for your full involvement.

A historic sports example is Donald Trump's involve-ment with the United States Football League. "If there was a single miscalculation I made with the USFL, it was evaluating the strength of my fellow owners," said Trump. He was prepared for a long battle with the NFL, hopefully ending in a merger of the USFL (including his New Jersey Generals) with the NFL. As the league was disbanding and after the allocated finances of the league's owners were exhausted, Trump found that he was virtually alone in wanting to continue to battle the NFL. His lesson: check the depth of your partners' pockets before you venture with them. Also, make sure your partners' hearts to pursue the endeavor are as big as yours. If Trump had more information on the latter, he might never have taken the interest in the upstart league.

Move cautiously in hiring representatives, in representing someone yourself, or in entering into a relationship in which you will be affected by the business decisions of others.

⇥ Takeaways ⇤

1. Know that you are compatible with your agent or employer.
2. Understand that compatibility does not mean sharing the same style.
3. Align interests and remove conflicts.
4. Select the right agent.
5. As a principal, manage the agent.
6. As an agent, manage the principal.
7. Manage expectations.

CHAPTER 8

KNOW YOUR AUDIENCE

Dog fighting is a terrible thing. . . . I offer my
deepest apologies to everybody . . .

—Michael Vick, former NFL quarterback

"Well, sir, I'm not here to talk about the past."
Mark McGwire responded carefully with the
words his lawyers crafted and sounded more and more like
a very good politician. "I'm here to talk about the positive."
Though McGwire may not have realized it, the subject of
the conversation wasn't steroids, but maintaining his positive celebrity status. It was March 17, 2005.

"I don't know," McGwire continued, alluding to baseball's then current steroids scandal, "I'm a retired player."
Snickers erupted in the small Hearing Room 254 in the
old Rayburn House Office Building. McGwire looked
uncomfortable but stuck with his game plan—and his
story. Some representatives on the panel looked indignant.

Congressman Mark Souder of Indiana said, "This is what we do. We're an oversight committee. If Enron comes in here and says, 'We don't want to talk about the past,' do you think Congress is going to let them get away with that?" Suddenly, baseball's slugger-hero was being compared to America's most-hated megacorporation—and the audience took notice.

"I accept my attorney's advice not to comment on the issue." The response sounded lame, undoubtedly even to McGwire, but that's how his testimony ended.

All in all, it was a very bad day for McGwire—and America's national pastime. One congressman made noises about removing McGwire's name from a five-mile stretch of highway in Missouri, but the scar the incident inflicted would run far deeper than that.

McGwire lost that negotiation and still has not recovered. He could have said, "I tried performance-enhancing substances, and I should not have." He then could have added, "Kids, it's just not worth it. Your body is more important than any game. Your future is more important than any player." That would have made him a role model: not for breaking a record, not even for admitting that he had *cheated* to break a record, but for successfully negotiating his celebrity status with the public.

In their preparation, McGwire and his attorneys somehow lost sight of the fact that they were involved in a public negotiation—that his celebrity, the continued value of his image, and his signature on trading cards hinged on how he performed on stage that day. These oversized public negotiations often arise in crisis situations. In the midst of a crisis, it is important to be aware of the long-term effects of our actions and not just focus on the immediate resolution to the crisis. The public stage is a much bigger venue than most of us will encounter in our daily lives. But we must be mindful of the fact that we may have to negotiate in the public eye, no matter how remote that possibility may be.

⤙ COURT OF PUBLIC OPINION ⤚

When considering the issue of your audience, focus on the size and any special circumstances facing a particular audience in a given situation. We have talked extensively in this book about the style and relationship elements to consider when our counterpart is a single person or an enterprise. But what if our audience is neither? What if it is the public at large?

We can all take instruction from the sports world about public negotiations, but this type of negotiation happens outside the sports world too. You may recall the 1982 Tylenol murders where seven people died after ingesting poison-laced Extra Strength Tylenol. How could a company—in this case, Johnson & Johnson—convince the public that Tylenol was once again safe and that they could use it without fear? The first thing the company did was to recall $100 million worth of Tylenol. Next it put antitampering protections on the product. These swift actions by Johnson & Johnson made the scandal short lived.

The lesson of the Tylenol case is this: if a negative story about you is going to come out and you know at some point you will want to clear your good name, you need to act quickly and sincerely. Four sports examples give us the primary guidance on this issue: Mark McGwire, Kobe Bryant, Michael Vick, and Marion Jones.

In 1998, Major League Baseball needed *something* to draw fans back into stadiums after a rancorous and lengthy labor dispute had canceled the season's play. This was a *big* negotiation. Sometimes fate gives an assist, but no one could have predicted that in this case the assist would have been a giant, redheaded baseball player for the St. Louis Cardinals and a peace-sign-kissing Dominican slugger from the Chicago Cubs. But these unlikely saviors injected pure adrenaline into a moribund season by their race, head to head, to beat Roger Maris's record for the most home runs hit in a single season, 61 home runs. The redhead, Mark McGwire, won the contest with a still amazing but no longer record-holding 70 home runs. Baseball had in fact stumbled on a nice exchange with the public to draw fans back in. It was not known then that one member of the home-run tandem was going to have enormous problems and that his own public negotiation would fail.

When Sammy Sosa, the Dominican, and McGwire testified before the Congressional House Government

Onetime Major League Baseball home-run king Mark McGwire testifying before Congress in 2005

Reform Committee seven years later, Sosa—still an active player at the time—had not changed much physically, but the retired McGwire was balding and dramatically thinner. In the spirit of St. Patrick's Day, the now incongruously nicknamed "Big Mac" wore a light green tie. As the situation had been during their famous home-run competition, the two still had some surprises up their sleeves. While Sosa and another pro baseballer, Rafael Palmeiro, denied using steroids, McGwire essentially pleaded the "Fifth" and refused to answer the question. Palmeiro, who came to Miami from Cuba at age six, said, "I have never used steroids, period. I do not know how to say it any more clearly than that—never." Compared to Sosa's and Palmeiro's straight answers, McGwire's equivocation looked to many like a tacit admission of guilt.

At the time, of course, nobody knew that Palmeiro had recently tested positive for steroids (the results were not yet disclosed), and we all chose to forget that Sosa had been discovered using an illegal "corked" bat the previous season, giving him an unfair batting advantage. We should have known about Palmeiro because he spoke with such conviction—like Bill Clinton looking straight into the camera and denying that he'd "had sex with *that* woman," or the first George Bush telling us to read his lips when he promised "no new taxes." Like these politicians, McGwire had been a hero, then a disappointment, to many people. Now he was the only one struggling to find the high road out of a very difficult swamp.

⇥ THE APOLOGY ⇤

"I didn't force her to do anything against her will." An honest, direct, prompt, correctly delivered apology seems to take anyone a long way in terms of regaining public acceptance after a violation of public expectations. Pro basketball player Kobe Bryant began with more of an excuse than an apology, but then he began to deliver the right words: "I sit here in front of you furious at myself, disgusted at myself, for making a mistake of adultery. I love my wife with all my heart." He then turned; looked at his wife, Vanessa; and said, "You're a blessing. You're a piece of my heart. You're the air I breathe. And you're the strongest person I know. I'm sorry for having to put you through this and having to put our family through this." This was Kobe Bryant shortly after he was accused of having nonconsensual sex with a Vail, Colorado, hotel employee.

We all forgive people for their modest wrongdoings, particularly when they give us the quick, unequivocal apology. The vernacular has become "my bad." If that's delivered, we often move on as though nothing happened ... or at least we are more likely to do so.

In contrast, what we don't like is the cover-up—the "I did not have sexual relations with *that* woman" excuse. We can look to Michael Vick to lead us through that scenario. When people wondered why Vick volunteered to begin serving his jail sentence three weeks early, Daniel Richman, a Columbia law professor, said appropriately, "There's an audience beyond a judge."

Unlike Bryant and McGwire, who had committed few public faux pas and were high on the public love list, Michael Vick had been on a slippery slope. There were several extensively reported public violations before the most ominous connection with dog fighting.

Vick's athletic skill set was without equal. If he could ever immerse himself in a football system, or if one was molded specifically for him, there would be no stopping his team, the Atlanta Falcons of the NFL. However, the 2007 season may have been the perfect storm, bringing together this phenomenal talent and a new coach looking to make a strong impact. This combination ultimately prevented the team from realizing its aspirations.

The first reports only alluded to dog fights taking place at a property owned by superstar Vick. Ahhh, there had to be an explanation. Even though he had had a recent incident regarding possible marijuana possession at an airport and had given the fans the finger, this dog-fighting allegation was a bit much, even for this guy. After numerous opportunities to step forward, it was not until his guilt was apparent that Vick apologized for his role in a dog-fighting ring. The illegality was there in any event, but a more timely apology would have had a positive impact on his future with the many people involved in the legal process. Apparently, too, in private conversations with the NFL, Vick lied. Ultimately, all of this combined with the wrongdoing caused the temporary end to Vick's football career and his incarceration.

There is a stubbornness in some denials that does seem to be unique to athletes. Many people are familiar with the longtime denials of Major League Baseball's all-time home-run hitter Barry Bonds. No matter the strength of the allegations, Bonds has persevered in his denying the use of any performance-enhancing drugs. But his vehemence, other than the persistence of it, is dwarfed by that of cyclist Floyd Landis.

"I have never taken any banned substance, including testosterone," Landis asserted after he appeared to have won the Tour de France in 2006. "I was the strongest man at the Tour de France, and that is why I am the champion."

The denial is problematic enough. The proclamation that sometimes follows is even more troublesome. "I will fight these charges with the same determination and intensity that I bring to my training and racing. It is now my goal to clear my name and restore what I worked so hard to achieve." The difficulties in the Landis instance are the evidence against him, his rebuttal, and his vehemence.

Continued participation in the sport makes redemption easier, as Kobe Bryant has demonstrated. Vick, on the other hand, suffers from being incarcerated. As a result, he is unable to take part in his sport, and this makes it difficult, if not impossible, to clear his name with the public. Translated to a business environment this means that a company can continue its business after an apology. A coworker or family member can do likewise. The lesson is that there is power in a rapid admission of guilt followed by an apology; only then is it possible to move forward.

Former Olympic track star Marion Jones long denied any use of performance-enhancing drugs. She came under increased scrutiny not because her performance improved, but rather because of the negative revelations about the men in her life. First there was shot-putter husband C. J. Hunter, who competed at the Sydney Games. Then, later, there was sprinter Tim Montgomery, the father of her son, Monty. Both of these men were found to have been involved in the use of performance-enhancing drugs. Eventually Jones admitted to federal prosecutors that she too had been a user, and she was sentenced to six months in prison.

"It's with a great amount of shame that I stand before you and tell you that I have betrayed your trust," said Jones. "I have been dishonest and you have the right to be angry with me. . . . Therefore, I want to ask for your forgiveness for my actions, and I hope you can find it in your heart to forgive me." In the long run she probably will be better served for having said this, but she'll never reach her former level of fame. An earlier admission and apology might have allowed her to at least be partially rehabilitated. The apology was less effective because it came after years of denial and as a result of the threat of prosecution. Turning in her medals was also a positive step.

In so many instances the punishment that is most severe and that could have been avoided is the punishment for lying about the transgression. In these sports-related instances, such deceit has brought the athletes not only additional jail time but also a decreased earnings potential as a result of their being diminished in the eyes of the public. For you, the basic premise is the same: the sooner you can disclose negative issues and move on, the better off you are likely to be and the greater the likelihood of reviving whatever transaction you may be involved in.

EXPERT TIP

Where there has been a negative event, the client should apologize as quickly and concisely as possible.

— Rich Nichols, sports lawyer and
counsel to former Olympian Marion Jones

⊰ TIMING ⊱

Bad news does not get better with time. The sooner you are able to get bad news out, or at least to deliver it on your own terms, the less likely it is to harm your position in a way that you don't anticipate. The key, as my Chinatown stadium story in Chapter 7 illustrates, is making sure the news is delivered in the way that tells the story you want told. If you are deceptive or late with bad news, it can be devastating. If it is a negative event, as the Tylenol poisoning was, you also must clearly lay out your plan for corrective action.

By the time the Mitchell Report on steroids in baseball was released in early 2007, there was a road map for anyone accused—that is, *if* the athlete wanted to restore his or her public image. It seemed that if you were guilty, the right move was to admit it and apologize. It was becoming clear that the "I did not know" approach was ineffective, even if true.

Roger Clemens, the multiple Cy Young Award–winning pitcher and his teammate and training buddy Andy Pettitte decided to take two different approaches. (Of course, they may have had different levels of involvement.) Pettitte confessed to the accusations against him of using Human Growth Hormone. Clemens took the path of vehement denials. Pettitte is essentially done with the issue; for Clemens, discussion still rages, and the court of public opinion appears to be voting negatively on its image of him.

⇥ DELIVERING A POSITIVE MESSAGE ⇤

Negotiations in the public eye do not always involve bad news. The Beckham negotiation discussed in Chapter 5 illustrates one final point in thinking about your audience, particularly when your negotiation is facing public scrutiny. Beckham's signing with Major League Soccer (MLS) was one big public relations moment, which served as part of a long-term effort to garner public interest in the sport and ensure league viability. It was reminiscent of Pelé signing with the New York Cosmos of the old North American Soccer League (NASL) in 1975, and it signaled a message to the public about the league's strengths and goals. Although the NASL did fold in 1984, Pelé's presence for two years, including numerous historic moments in New York, proved beneficial. Pelé's negotiation said "support us," "we're good," and "we're going to be around." The same is true for a public company signing a deal, hiring a key employee, or gaining favorable financing. The message? We are here to stay, and we are strong.

Be aware that your negotiation often involves more than the one party across the table from you. The key is knowing first who you want your audience to be and then the size and any special circumstances related to it. Craft your message carefully, as your negotiation with a broader audience may be your most difficult one ever. These steps are applicable not only at the business level, but also for more personal interactions. Give full consideration to your audience.

⇥ TAKEAWAYS ⇤

1. Determine the size of the audience you are addressing or desire to address and its unique features.
2. Apologize as rapidly, sincerely, succinctly, and specifically as possible.
3. Understand that the public is smarter than you are.
4. Tell it all and move on.
5. Time your positive statements to serve your needs, and make your statements sooner rather later.
6. Don't get into any more trouble.

CHAPTER 9

NEGOTIATE LIKE A PRO

*If we play our game as well as we can, we can
beat an opponent no matter what he does.
We let them adjust to us, rather than we to them.*

—John Wooden

Winning certainly has a different meaning in every negotiation. Achieving that desired outcome is most likely to occur when we use all of the skills that we possess in a carefully prepared manner. A few years ago we were fortunate enough to host NBA commissioner David Stern at Wharton. He gave a speech to all of the negotiation classes being taught that term and shared his negotiating experiences with us. Following the speech, in a question-and-answer session, a female student asked: "Is it unfair for a woman to use tears in a negotiation?" His response was, "If I could, I would." Yes, it is fair to use all of the legitimate tools at your disposal.

How do you put all of the elements together? One of my colleagues at Wharton, Keith Weigelt, is a Taoist. He also likes sports and has worked with athletes over the years. I have had him come in to talk with NFL players about strategy and negotiating. He likes to recommend that they read *The Book of Five Rings*, one of those classic books on military and conflict strategy, written in 1645, that can be applied to business. The one key point that Weigelt pulls from the Taoist philosophy and that applies both on the field of play and in the business arena is to maintain a normal state of mind. The magic of success really comes when you are able to practice exactly in the manner that you play. The trick is to practice with the same intensity that you use when you play, but also to play the game with the same relatively relaxed frame of mind that you have in practice. That is the challenge. Can you make free throws in the gym with no one else around? Can you make the same shots with a full-capacity crowd to win the world championship? Many of us are great at the driving range, but how many of us can transfer that to the course on Saturday morning? It is rare to be able to do so. The important point is that you must be prepared. Do the "practice" phase as thoroughly as possible.

"Our players are told over and over again that I am not worried about our opponents, but about what we will do ourselves," Wooden reflects on his coaching days. "They are told everything will be fine if, at the end of every game, each boy can honestly answer to himself that he did his best to be prepared for the game and did his best in the game."

If you've taken in what this book has to offer, you should now be an even better negotiator. If you apply it, better still; if you practice it fully, you'll be the best you can be. And as Coach Wooden told us in the beginning, what more can you do? Remember, he won an unmatchable 10 NCAA basketball championships, so he knows what he is talking about.

Coach Pat Summitt expands upon Wooden: "Sometimes the best-laid plan doesn't work, and sometimes, you don't have a plan at all, and things work out beautifully. Most of the time, you have only half a plan, and it about half works. But every once in a while, a good plan works to utter perfection. When that happens, you don't write it off to luck or good fortune. You examine it, and ask yourself why things turned out so well."

Sure, we have all had success without a plan, without thorough preparation. But we are more likely to have success in negotiating with a plan than without one—with a plan that incorporates the lessons in this book. And when the plan works, learn from it. Use it to win again. If the plan does not work, learn from that too, and do not repeat the same mistakes.

So where do we end up? With the lesson so many of us heard from our parents: do the best you can. You will know you are doing that when you combine all of the elements laid out in this book. Your best gets even better if your preparation is done at the highest level. You are not doing the best you can if you have not fully prepared.

Pat Summitt, women's basketball coach at the University
of Tennessee

EXPERT TIP

Winning can be defined as the science
of being totally prepared.

—George Allen

After all the proper steps have been taken, it will sometimes become clear that a good deal cannot be made. The only deal available may be a bad one or one that's not in your best interest. If things get to that point, will you make the right decision? There are certainly those times when the right deal is no deal. If you are properly prepared, you will recognize those times. You will walk away because you properly planned in advance where that breakpoint is.

Occasionally, I've been involved in selecting for a client the best negotiator available, or in advising a client whom to select. A few years ago my client was NFL star Kellen Winslow II. "Ken, I want you to represent my son." I could not have been more flattered than when I heard these words from my longtime friend, former student, and business partner Kellen Winslow Sr. The family had made the decision for their son Kellen (K2) to leave the University of Miami early and enter the NFL draft.

I sat in my office at Wharton looking out the window toward West Philadelphia. "Kellen, I can't tell you how much I appreciate this, but for all kinds of reasons, I just can't."

The biggest logistical reason was that I had not been certified by the NFL Players Association for years. Key, too, was that I was not at a point where I was intimately familiar with NFL salaries. In some ways, with K2, the latter obstacle would not have been that tough to overcome. He was going to be a top-10 pick in the draft.

"Kellen, I'm sorry," I replied, "but let me know if I can be helpful along the way."

A couple of days later, Kellen called me back and said that he was trying to put together an agent selection panel for his son and that he wanted me to be a part of it. The process is ultracompetitive. Agents pursue the top collegiate athletes in order to represent them in the draft and get paid approximately 3 percent of the athletes' salaries for doing so. In this process of agents wooing players, some frowned-upon favors are delivered, including cash payments and illegal inducements, such as prostitutes and drugs. Kellen Sr. knew about the seamy process from firsthand experience as both a player and an agent. He wanted to protect his son as much as possible.

His plan was to select a small number of agents to come to Miami to interview with a panel that would include Kellen; K2; a financial advisor, Pete Shaw; K2's best friend, Chris; and me.

It was a fascinating process since we were looking for someone who, among other things, was the best negotiator. For me, I was listening largely to gauge the agents' preparation. They all had success records. How far had they gone in the process of preparing for their negotiations with K2 without even having the deal in hand?

Even more so, the crucial questions in the selection process for me really were not related to the contract negotiation. They were: How well had the agents prepared for this meeting with the panel, and did they display their preparation effectively? How seriously had they taken it? Had they recognized that they were entering a negotiation by coming into this boardroom?

For me, the key question for the agents was this: "Will you cut your fees?" Their answer was actually less important than the preparation they demonstrated for this interview, which was, in fact, a huge negotiation with the panelists. In a competitive process they had to contemplate that *price* was going to be one of the criteria the panel would focus on. To me and the panel, that was reflective of their process, and we did not want a lack of preparation when it came to doing the ultimate deal. (K2 selected the agent he was personally most comfortable with and ended up being the sixth overall pick in the draft by the Cleveland Browns.)

One overriding lesson in this book about negotiating comes from the step that Alex Rodriguez took: ask for help. Our bargaining styles and experiences lock us into particular approaches. It is difficult for any of us to move out of our comfort zones or to envision approaches that we are not accustomed to. If you have resources that you can pursue for advice, do so. As we saw in Chapter 1, Bob Johnson, one of the richest men in America, did just that. Ultimately, only you can make the decision to seek advice, but the more input you are able to receive without negatively impacting your bargain, the better off you are likely to be.

Another one of the richest men in America has been a baseball fan since he was eight and took a train from Omaha to Chicago to see the Cubs play the Dodgers to a 9–9 tie in 19 innings. Other than his doing that and saying that purchasing a team is a bad investment, it's tough to justify his finding his way into this book. But here he is again delivering a message that applies to any negotiation. Warren Buffett is known for his simple advice: invest in products you know and understand. In negotiating this translates to: focus on relationships. Often we need only strip whatever negotiation we are involved in down to its bare, most human foundation. Communicate to the other side directly why you need what you need. Before you do this, though, you must have confidence that the appropriate relationship has been established between you and your counterpart. Once it is, know that none other than Warren Buffett has advised you that your instinct to connect on the most personal level is important and may be the way to close your deal, even if you thought the deal was lost.

There is no question that some of us have better negotiating skills than others. But first, know that the other side may not have taken the same steps in preparing that you have. As we noted, by the time Bill Walsh got to Joe Montana, he had made stars out of quarterbacks with nowhere near Montana's talent by having them prepare thoroughly and having them use other strategies that were known to work. Virgil Carter, Steve DeBerg, and Jack Kemp were obscure quarterbacks elevated to the highest levels of success, even if only for a season or two. Without the correct system—preparing thoroughly, knowing their opponents' tendencies and goals, and anticipating the worst case—they would not have reached those heights.

Going forward, begin with the Negotiation Game Plan Worksheet (see Chapter 1). That, guided by the stories on the pages of this book, should lead you to better negotiation outcomes.

⇥ FINAL TAKEAWAYS ⇤

Negotiate Like a Pro

1. Prepare with passion.
2. Stick with *your* style.
3. Set goals and aim high.
4. Seek out leverage, but don't lie.
5. Focus on the value of relationships.
6. Embrace the bargaining process.
7. Know your audience.
8. Play smart.

BARGAINING STYLES ASSESSMENT TOOL

(Reprinted with permission from G. Richard Shell, *Bargaining for Advantage: Negotiation Strategies for Reasonable People,* Appendix A [New York, Penguin, 2nd edition, 2006].)

Follow this process to determine your personal bargaining style preferences.

1. Without giving the matter too much thought (and without revising your answers for any reason!), please select ONE STATEMENT in each pair of statements below. Select the statement you think is *more accurate* for you when you face a negotiation or disagreement with someone else—even if you think neither statement is very accurate or both are very accurate. Think about such situations in general—not just ones at work or at home. And don't pick the statement you "ought" to agree with; pick the one your gut tells you is more accurate for

you most of the time. Some statements repeat, but do not worry about answering consistently. Just keep going. All answers are equally "correct."

2. After selecting a statement from every pair, go back and add up the total number of As, Bs, Cs, Ds, and Es you recorded. Put the totals in the "Results" space at the end of the survey.

3. Return to Chapter 2 for an explanation of your scores and the general subject of bargaining styles.

STEP 1: STYLE SURVEY

1. E. I work hard to preserve the relationship with my counterpart
    B. I try to identify the underlying issues
    I select __e__

2. D. I work to defuse tense situations
    A. I gain concessions by being persistent
    I select __A__

3. E. I focus on solving the other party's problem
    D. I try to avoid unnecessary conflicts
    I select __e__

4. C. I search for a fair compromise
    E. I work hard to preserve the relationship
    I select __C__

5. C. I suggest fair compromises
    D. I avoid personal confrontations
    I select __C__

6. C. I seek the midpoint between our positions
    B. I search for the problems underlying our disagreements
    I select __B__

7. D. I tactfully resolve many disagreements
    C. I expect "give and take" in negotiations
    I select __C__

8. A. I clearly communicate my goals
    B. I focus my attention on the other side's needs
    I select __A__

9. D. I prefer to put off confrontations with other
        people
    A. I win my points by making strong arguments
    I select __A__

10. C. I am usually willing to compromise
    A. I enjoy winning concessions
    I select __C__

11. B. I candidly address all the problems between us
    E. I care more about the relationship than winning
        the last concession
    I select __E__

12. D. I try to avoid unnecessary personal conflicts
    C. I search for fair compromises
    I select __C__

13. C. I give concessions and expect some concessions in
         return
     A. I strive to achieve all my goals in negotiations
     I select __A__

14. A. I enjoy getting concessions more than making
         them
     E. I strive to maintain the relationship
     I select __E__

15. E. I accommodate their needs to preserve the
         relationship
     D. I leave confrontational situations to others if I can
     I select __E__

16. E. I try to address the other person's needs
     A. I work hard to achieve all my goals
     I select __A__

17. A. I make sure to discuss my goals
     D. I emphasize areas on which we agree
     I select __D__

18. E. I am looking out for the relationship
     C. I give concessions and expect the other side to do
         the same
     I select __C__

19. B. I identify and discuss all of our differences
    D. I try to avoid confrontations
    I select B

20. A. I obtain my share of concessions
    E. I strive to maintain relationships
    I select E

21. B. I identify and discuss all of our differences
    C. I look for the compromises that might bridge the
       gap
    I select C

22. E. I develop good relations with the other guy
    B. I develop options that address both of our needs
    I select E

23. C. I seek the middle ground
    A. I strive to achieve my goals in negotiations
    I select A

24. B. I identify all of our differences and look for
       solutions
    D. I try to avoid unnecessary conflicts
    I select B

25. E. I try to preserve the relationship with my
        counterpart
     C. I search for fair compromises
     I select _C_

26. D. I emphasize the issues on which we agree
     B. I uncover and address the things on which we
        disagree
     I select _B_

27. A. I work hard to achieve my goals
     B. I pay attention to the other person's needs
     I select _A_

28. C. I look for the fair compromise
     B. I try to identify all of the underlying probems
     I select _B_

29. D. I avoid unnecessary disagreements
     B. I focus on solving the other person's problem
     I select _D_

30. A. I strive to achieve my goals
     B. I work to address everyone's needs
     I select _A_

STEP 2: RECORD RESULTS

Add up all your A, B, C, D, and E answers on the previous pages and put those totals below:

As = _____8_____

Bs = _____5_____

Cs = _____7_____

Ds = _____2_____

Es = _____8_____

_____30_____ TOTAL (Must equal 30!)

Now, return to Chapter 2.

NOTES

⇥ Introduction: How and Why ⇤
to Use This Book

1   "If you don't know where you're going, you'll end up somewhere else." (Horn, p. 11)

⇥ Chapter 1: Prepare with Passion ⇤

11   "Failing to prepare is preparing to fail." (Wooden with Jamison, p. 58)

14   "The key to successfully meeting with him [Castro] is to remember that he is a monologist," often [talking] nonstop for an hour or two." (Ueberroth, p. 296)

23   "Bob, continue to do whatever you are doing, keeping things low key, and continue to play the game." (Benoliel and Cashdan, p. 124)

24   "Once you have analyzed your own position, there is a person on the other side of the table who is going to be really tough, and you have to analyze his or her position as well." (Falk, p. 341)

25   "Gentlemen, today we're going to figure out how to put our shoes and socks on." (Horowitz)

26   "Otherwise we would not be doing everything possible to *prepare* in the best way." (Wooden with Jamison, p. 61)

26   Wooden conveyed complete confidence in his team via his steadfast refusal to call a time-out in the final minutes of a game. (Sonny Vaccaro, telephone interview, Philadelphia, February 15, 2008) (Gergen)

27   "I believe there is nothing wrong with the other fellow being better than you are if you've prepared and are functioning in the way you've tried to prepare." (Wooden with Jamison, p. 29).

28   "Despite my longevity in the sports representation business, I always prepare thoroughly." (Falk, p. 333)

28   "Champions are champions not because they do anything extraordinary but because they do the ordinary things better than anyone else." (Dungy with Whitaker, p. 43)

29   "I'm looking for uncommon people because we want to be successful, not average." (Dungy with Whitaker, p. 29)

29   "Steve Kerr of the Chicago Bulls shot five hundred free throws a day to make himself uncommon." (Dungy with Whitaker, p. 29)

32   ". . . including the desperate ones at the end of a game when we may have only one chance to pull out a victory." (Rapaport, p. 110)

⭑ CHAPTER 2: STICK WITH *YOUR* STYLE ⭑

35   "It's not how you play that matters—it's whether you win; it's whether you're number one." (Allen, p. 45)

42   "I hate to lose more than I like to win." ("When Losing Becomes a Habit")

48   "I think you have to treat players intelligently." (King, p. 57)

55   "Come on in, Mr. Parker." (Parker relayed this story in a meeting several years ago; the quotes are my recollection of the story)

⭑ CHAPTER 3: SET GOALS AND AIM HIGH ⭑

57   "I decided to set a $4 million floor for each potential sponsor. Establishing a floor, or a minimum, is a negotiating concept that has always worked for me." (Ueberroth, p. 61)

57   "This separates the serious businessmen from the phonies who want to take part in something just for the sake of it and from those looking for a cheap opportunity." (Ueberroth, p. 63)

60   Ironically, one of the best visualizers is basketball all-star Allen Iverson. (Larry Platt analyzes this best in *Only the Strong Survive: The Odyssey of Allen Iverson*, Harper Entertainment, New York, 2003. For the more formal psychology of this, see Robert Cialdini.)

63   "There is nothing more powerful than for me to genuinely have the power to walk away if I can't

get what I feel is right." (Tony Agnone, telephone interview, March 22, 2008)

64   "A stalemate is a great alternative to a bad deal." (Arn Tellem, speech at the Wharton School, Philadelphia, November 7, 2007)

66   His then team, the Orix BlueWave, clearly understood this. (Chass)

67   The $51.1 million fee the team received dwarfed its payroll that year, which was only $17 million. ("Bargaining at Fever Pitch," p. 5)

68   "Our goal every year is to win a title." (Summitt and Jenkins, p. xv)

69   ". . . just after placing a bet, they are much more confident of their horse's chances of winning than they are immediately before laying down that bet." (Cialdini, p. 69)

72   Movies, television shows, and newspaper and magazine articles are always about the exchanges, the old smoke-filled rooms, and the final late-night meetings. (Benjamin)

⇥ CHAPTER 4: SEEK LEVERAGE ⇤

75   "This is for Rudy." (*Rudy*, TriStar Pictures, 1993)

75   "I'll pay you $5 million" must have been the words Don King uttered. (Newfield, p. 61, for details of this transaction)

77   "This was the opportunity of a lifetime for Don King." (Newfield, p. 56)

86   "I don't think there is a general manager in baseball that believes him when he says he has other teams interested." (Benoliel and Cashdan, p. 117)

86   He actually incorporates this into one of his 12 essential rules: convince the other side that you have an option. (Steinberg and D'Orso, p. 225)

86   "Maintain your integrity." (Jared Bartie, telephone interview, March 22, 2008)

86   "A gold medal is a wonderful thing, but if you're not enough without it, you'll never be enough with it." (*Cool Runnings*, Disney, 1993)

88   "I don't want to be a jerk or anything." (Callahan)

91   "If we don't resolve this today, we won't discuss it with you again until the season is over." (Stanley King, telephone interview, February 15, 2008)

93   "Why are they potentially interested?" (Phil de Picciotto, telephone interview, April 22, 2008)

94   "Al should just say, 'Gentlemen, I'll take the Rosenbloom deal.'" (Harris, p. 431)

⇨ CHAPTER 5: FOCUS ON RELATIONSHIPS AND INTERESTS ⇦

97   "I'm excited to go to a team that has a lot of drivers I can learn from and who know how to win." ("Danica to Stay in IRL But Switch to Andretti Green Racing")

97   "Next question?" (Smith)

103 "For Americans doing a business deal, it's 'Let's do the deal and go.'" (Ming and Bucher, p. 101)

105 "I got a call from a firm in Japan first asking me if I knew who Matsui was." (Tellem speech)

108 "Talk to the Yankees directly, without your agent." (Kelly and Cimilluca, p. 1)

109 He did not because he wanted to enable the Penguins to sign more young talent in order to become more competitive. (Molinari)

110 "I want to win in IndyCar." ("Danica to Stay in IRL But Switch to Andretti Green Racing")

112 David Beckham had his self-interest in mind. ("David Beckham's Potential U.S. Move Could Give MLS Glitz")

112 "I said, 'There may be an opportunity.'" ("Selig Gives Blessing to Mega-Merger")

⇥ CHAPTER 6: EMBRACE THE ⇤
BARGAINING PROCESS

119 "I've been playing baseball for a long time . . . every time I've heard the umpire get ready to start a game, he always says, 'Play ball!' I've never once heard him say, 'Work ball.'"(Dungy and Whitaker, p. 49)

119 "On the big deals, I like to meet in person initially." (de Picciotto interview)

120 "You're the experts; you know the market." (Shapiro and Jankowski, p. 147)

121 "Knowing where you want to end up is easy to prepare, the hard part is how to get there. That is the more important, difficult part." (de Picciotto interview)

123 "Above all, the experience of going undefeated . . ."
      (Summitt and Jenkins, p. xv)

127 "When I worked at the Upper Deck Company, I
      was negotiating a royalty deal against the agent for a
      big-name player." W. David Cornwell, speech at the
      Wharton School, Philadelphia, April 15, 2008)

130 "To seduce almost anyone, ask for and listen to his [or
      her] opinion." (Horn, p. 18)

130 "You should remain silent to the point of discomfort."
      (Cornwell speech)

131 "At some point in every negotiation you have to say
      where you are going, and then there's no more. Otherwise
      there won't be any resolution." (David Stern, speech at
      the Wharton School, Philadelphia, April 9, 2003)

135 "Don't be too concerned with regard to things over
      which you have no control, because that will eventually
      have an adverse effect on things over which you have
      control." (Horowitz)

⊰ CHAPTER 7: HANDLE OTHER ⊱
PEOPLE'S BUSINESS

137 "That's what agents are for." (Shropshire and Davis,
      p. 22)

138 I relayed an apocryphal story about Green Bay Packers
      coach Vince Lombardi and his 1960s view of agents.
      (Shropshire and Davis, p. 12)

144 The leading scholarly article on the topic is called "When
      Should We Use Agents?" (Rubin and Sanders, p. 401)

147 "The key is to make certain that your client knows where the deal is likely to end up, . . ." (Bill Strickland, telephone interview, May 1, 2008)

148 "If there was a single miscalculation I made with the USFL, it was evaluating the strength of my fellow owners." (Trump and Schwartz, p. 277)

⇥ CHAPTER 8: KNOW YOUR AUDIENCE ⇤

151 "Dog fighting is a terrible thing. . . . I offer my deepest apologies to everybody . . ." ("Verbatim")

151 "Well, sir, I'm not here to talk about the past." ("McGwire Mum on Steroids in Hearing")

156 "I didn't force her to do anything against her will." (Madigan)

157 "I sit here in front of you furious at myself, disgusted at myself, for making a mistake of adultery." (Wise, Mike, and Alex Markels, "Lakers' Star Bryant Is Charged with Sex Assault at Colorado Spa," July 19, 2003, query.nytimes.com/gst/fullpage.html?res=9F05 E2DF1E3CF93AA25754C0A9659C8B63)

157 "There's an audience beyond a judge." ("Perspectives")

158 Apparently, too, in private conversations with the NFL, Vick lied. ("Sentence Puts Vick's NFL Career in Jeopardy")

159 "I have never taken any banned substance, including testosterone." (Macur)

160 "It's with a great amount of shame that I stand before you and tell you that I have betrayed your trust." (Zinser and Schmidt)

161 "Where there has been a negative event, the client should apologize as quickly and concisely as possible." (Rich Nichols, telephone interview, May 1, 2008)

⇥ CHAPTER 9: NEGOTIATE LIKE A PRO ⇤

165 "If we play our game as well as we can, we can beat an opponent no matter what he does." ("The Wooden Style")

165 "If I could, I would." (David Stern, speech at the Wharton School, Philadelphia, April 9, 2003)

166 "They are told everything will be fine if, at the end of every game, each boy can honestly answer to himself that he did his best to be prepared for the game and did his best in the game." (Wooden, *Practical Modern Basketball*, p. 47)

167 "Sometimes the best-laid plan doesn't work, . . ." (Summitt and Jenkins, p. xii)

169 "Winning can be defined as the science of being totally prepared." (Shapiro and Jankowski, p. 97)

BIBLIOGRAPHY

Allen, Jennifer. *Fifth Quarter: The Scrimmage of a Football Coach's Daughter*. New York: Random House, 2000.

Babcock, Linda, and Sarah Laschever. *Women Don't Ask: Negotiation and the Gender Divide*. Princeton, NJ: Princeton University Press, 2003.

"Bargaining at Fever Pitch," *Negotiation*, Vol. 3, No. 9, September 2007, p. 5.

Bazerman, Max H., and Margaret A. Neale. *Negotiating Rationally*. New York: The Free Press, 1992.

Benjamin, Matthew, "Go-To Guy: Agent Scott Boras Is Changing the Business of Baseball," *U.S. News & World Report*, May 2, 2004, www.usnews.com/usnews/biztech/articles/040510/10eeagent_3.htm.

Benoliel, Michael, Ed.D., and Linda Cashdan. *Done Deal: Interviews with the World's Best Negotiators*. Avon, MA: Adams Media, 2005.

Brockman, John, ed. *What Are You Optimistic About? Today's Leading Thinkers on Why Things Are Good and Getting Better*. New York: Edge Foundation, 2007.

Callahan, Tom. "Two Way Elway Gets His Way," May 16, 1983, www.time.com/time/magazine/article/0,9171, 925961,00.html.

Chass, Murray. "Mariners Gain Rights to Sign Suzuki," *New York Times*, November 10, 2000, query.nytimes. com/gst/fullpage.html?res=9E05E6DC1438F933A25 752C1A9669C8B63.

Cialdini, Robert B., Ph.D. *Influence: The Psychology of Persuasion.* New York: HarperCollins Publishers, 2007.

Clayton, John, "Sentence Puts Vick's NFL Career in Jeopardy," ESPN.com, December 10, 2007, sports. espn.go.com/nfl/columns/story?columnist=clayton_ john&id=3148767.

"Danica to Stay in IRL But Switch to Andretti Green Racing," July 26, 2006, sports.espn.go.com/rpm/news/ story?seriesId=1&id=2529364.

"David Beckham's Potential U.S. Move Could Give MLS Glitz," Foxnews.com, July 1, 2006, www.foxnews .com/story/0,2933,201803,00.html.

Dell, Donald L. *Minding Other People's Business: Winning Big for Your Clients and Yourself.* New York: Random House, 1989.

Donaldson, Michael C. *Fearless Negotiating: The Wish-Want-Walk Method to Reaching Agreements That Work.* New York: McGraw-Hill, 2007.

Dungy, Tony, and Norman Whitaker. *Quiet Strength: Principles, Practices and Priorities of a Winning Life.* Carol Stream, IL: Tyndale, 2007.

Falk, David. "The Art of Contract Negotiation,"
    Marquette Sports Law Journal, Vol. 3, No. 1, Fall 1992,
    pp. 331–360.

Fisher, Roger, and William Ury. *Getting to Yes: Negotiating
    Without Giving In.* New York: Penguin, 1981.

Freund, James C. *Smart Negotiating: How to Make Good
    Deals in the Real World.* New York: Simon & Schuster,
    1992.

Gergen, Joe. "The Rise of UCLA–1964," sportingnews.
    com, www.sportingnews.com/archives/ncaa/1964
    .html#top.

Harris, David. *The League: The Rise and Decline of the
    NFL.* New York: Bantam, 1986.

Heinrichs, Jay. *Thank You for Arguing: What Aristotle,
    Lincoln, and Homer Simpson Can Teach Us About the
    Art of Persuasion.* New York: Three Rivers Press, 2007.

Hoch, Stephen J., Howard C. Kunreuther, and Robert E.
    Gunther, eds. *Wharton on Making Decisions.* New
    York: John Wiley & Sons, 2001.

Hooper, Andy, and agencies. "RFU and Premier Rugby
    Announce New Deal," *Daily Telegraph*, UK, Novem-
    ber 15, 2007, www.telegraph.co.uk/sport/main
    .jhtml?xml=/sport/2007/11/15/urprem115.xml
    (accessed April 29, 2008).

Horn, Sam. *Pop: Stand Out in Any Crowd.* New York:
    Penguin, 2006.

Horowitz, Mitch. "From the Socks Up: The Extraordinary
    Coaching Life of John Wooden," www
    .mitchhorowitz.com/john-wooden.html.

"How to Negotiate Practically Anything," *Inc.*, February 1989, p. 35.

Huntsman, Jon M. *Winners Never Cheat: Everyday Values We Learned as Children (But May Have Forgotten)*. Philadelphia: Wharton School Publishing, 2005.

Kelly, Kate, and Dana Cimilluca. "Alex Rodriguez Gets a Surprise Assist from Fan in Omaha," *Wall Street Journal*, November 17–18, 2007, p. 1.

King, Peter. "Bill Walsh, 1931–2007," *Sports Illustrated*, August 8, 2007, p. 57.

Lewicki, Roy J., and Alexander Hiam. *Mastering Business Negotiation: A Working Guide to Making Deals & Resolving Conflict*. San Francisco: Jossey-Bass, 2006.

Lewis, Michael. *The Blind Side: Evolution of a Game*. New York: W. W. Norton & Company, 2007.

Lum, Grande. *The Negotiation Fieldbook: Simple Strategies to Help You Negotiate Everything*. New York: McGraw-Hill, 2005.

Macur, Juliet. "Testosterone Seems to Be Enhancer of Choice," *New York Times*, July 31, 2006, www.nytimes .com/2006/07/31/sports/31drugs.html?_ r=1&scp=1&sq=I%20have%20never%20taken%20 any%20banned%20substance,%20including%20 testosterone%20landis&st=cse&oref=slogin.

Madden, John, and David Anderson. *All Madden: Hey I'm Talking Pro Football!* New York: Red Bear, 1996.

Madigan, Nick. "Bryant Shows Up and Says Little," *New York Times*, August 7, 2005, query.nytimes.com/gst/

fullpage.html?res=9C04E5DB1731F934A3575BC0A
9659C8B63&sec=&spon=&scp=1&sq=&st=cse.

Malhotra, Deepak, and Max H. Bazerman. *Negotiation Genius*. New York: Bantam Books, 2007.

"McGwire Mum on Steroids in Hearing," CNN.com, March 17, 2005, www.cnn.com/2005/ ALLPOLITICS/03/17/steroids.baseball/index.html.

Ming, Yao, with Ric Bucher. *Yao: A Life in Two Worlds*. New York: Hyperion, 2004.

Mnookin, Robert H., Scott R. Peppet, and Andrew S. Tulumello. *Beyond Winning: Negotiating to Create Value in Deals and Disputes*. Cambridge, MA: Belknap Press of Harvard University Press, 2000.

Molinari, David. "Crosby's Negotiations Will Be Complex," *Pittsburgh Post Gazette*, July 5, 2007, www .post-gazette.com/pg/07192/800800-61.stm.

Newfield, Jack. *The Life and Crimes of Don King: The Shame of Boxing in America*. Harbor Electronic Publishing, 2003.

"Perspectives," *Newsweek*, December 3, 2007, p. 29.

Rapaport, Richard. "To Build a Winning Team: An Interview with Head Coach Bill Walsh," *Harvard Business Review*, p. 110, January 2993/February 1993.

Reardon, Kathleen. *Becoming a Skilled Negotiator*. Hoboken, NJ: John Wiley, 2005.

Rosenhaus, Drew, and Don Yaeger. *A Shark Never Sleeps: Wheeling and Dealing with the NFL's Most Ruthless Agent*. New York: Atria, 1998.

Rubin, Jeffrey Z., and Frank E. A. Sander. "When Should We Use Agents?: Direct vs. Representative Negotiation," *Negotiation Journal,* October 1988, p. 401.

"Selig Gives Blessing to Mega-Merger," ESPN.com, February 14, 2004, sports.espn.go.com/mlb/news/story?id=1735937.

Shapiro, Ronald, and Mark A. Jankowski with James Dale. *The Power of Nice: How to Negotiate So Everyone Wins—Especially You!* Revised edition. New York: John Wiley, 2001.

Shell, G. Richard. *Bargaining for Advantage: Negotiation Strategies for Reasonable People,* second edition. New York: Viking Penguin, 2006.

Shropshire, Kenneth, and Timothy Davis. *The Business of Sports Agents,* second edition. Philadelpha: University of Pennsylvania Press, 2008.

Smith, Michael. "McNabb: T. O. Situation Was about Money, Power," ESPN.com, February 2, 2006, sports.espn.go.com/nfl/news/story?id=1315565.

Spence, Gerry. *How to Argue and Win Every Time.* New York: St. Martin's Griffin, 1995.

Steinberg, Leigh, and Michael D'Orso. *Winning with Integrity: Getting What You Want Without Selling Your Soul.* New York: Three Rivers Press, 1998.

Stone, Douglas, Bruce Patton, and Sheila Heen. *Difficult Conversations: How to Discuss What Matters Most.* New York: Penguin Books, 1999.

Summitt, Pat, and Sally Jenkins. *Reach for the Summit: The Definite Dozen System for Succeeding at Whatever You Do.* New York: Broadway Books, 1998.

Thomas-Killman instrument, www.cpp.com/products/tki/index.asp.

Trope, Mike, and Steve Delsohn. *Necessary Roughness: The Other Game of Football Exposed by Its Most Controversial Superagent.* New York: Contemporary Books, 1987.

Trump, Donald J., and Tony Schwartz. *Trump: The Art of the Deal.* New York: Warner Books, 1987.

"The Tylenol Murders," History.com, www.history.com/this-day-in-history.do?action=VideoArticle&id=52868.

Ueberroth, Peter, with Richard Levin and Amy Quinn. *Made in America: His Own Story.* New York: William Morrow and Company, 1985.

Ury, William. *Getting Past No: Negotiating Your Way from Confrontation to Cooperation.* New York: Bantam Books, 1993.

____. *The Power of a Positive No: How to Say No and Still Get to Yes.* New York: Bantam Books, 2007.

"Verbatim," *Philadelphia Inquirer*, September 2, 2007, p. D3. Williams, Terrie, and Joe Cooney. *The Personal Touch: What You Really Need to Succeed in Today's Fast-paced Business World.* New York: Warner Books, 1994.

"When Losing Becomes a Habit," The Hindu, December 1, 2006, www.hindu.com/2006/12101/stories/2006120107292200.htm.

Wise, Mike, and Alex Markels, "Lakers' Star Bryant Is Charged With Sex Assault at Colorado Spa," July 19, 2003. query.nytimes.com/gst/fullpage.html?res=9F05E2DF1E3CF93AA25754C0A9659C8B63.

Wooden, John R. *Practical Modern Basketball*, second edition. New York: John Wiley & Sons, 1966.

Wooden, John, with Steve Jamison. *Wooden: A Lifetime of Observations and Reflections On and Off the Court.* New York: McGraw-Hill, 1997.

Wooden, John, and Steve Jamison. *The Essential Wooden: Lifetime of Lessons on Leaders and Leadership.* New York: McGraw-Hill, 2007.

"The Wooden Style," *Time*, February 12, 1973, p. 2, www.time.com/time/magazine/article/0,9171, 903847-2,00.html.

Woolf, Bob. *Behind Closed Doors*. New York: Atheneum, 1976.

Zinser, Lynn, and Michael S. Schmidt. "Jones Admits to Doping and Enters Guilty Plea," *New York Times*, October 6, 2007, www.nytimes.com/2007/10/06/sports/othersports/06balco.html?scp=1&sq=%93It%92s+with+a+great+amount+of+shame+that+I+stand+before+you++marion+jones&st=nyt.

INDEX

ABOUT THE AUTHOR

Kenneth L. Shropshire is the David W. Hauck Professor at the Wharton School of the University of Pennsylvania, director of its Wharton Sports Business Initiative, and academic director for Wharton's Business Management and Entrepreneurial Program for NFL players. Shropshire joined the Wharton faculty in 1986 and specializes in negotiations and sports business. He teaches the Negotiation and Dispute Resolution course both at Wharton's main campus in Philadelphia and at Wharton West in San Francisco and to executives around the world.

Shropshire is a former president of the largest organization of attorneys in the sports business, the Sports Lawyers Association. He also serves as an arbitrator for the National Football League Players Association (NFLPA) and USA Track & Field federation (USATF).

After receiving an undergraduate degree in economics from Stanford University and law degree from Columbia University Law School, Shropshire practiced law in Los Angeles and later served as an executive with the Los Angeles Olympic Organizing Committee leading up to the 1984 Olympics.

www.kennethshropshire.com